James & John Stuart Mill
ON
EDUCATION

Landmarks in the History of Education

James & John Stuart Mill
ON
EDUCATION

Edited by

F. A. CAVENAGH

GREENWOOD PRESS, PUBLISHERS
WESTPORT, CONNECTICUT

Library of Congress Cataloging in Publication Data

Cavenagh, Francis Alexander, 1884-1946, comp.
  James & John Stuart Mill on education.

    Reprint of the 1931 ed. published at the University
Press, Cambridge, Eng., issued in series: Landmarks
in the history of education.
    Bibliography: p.
    1. Education--Philosophy. 2. Mill, James, 1773-
1836. Article on education. 3. Mill, John Stuart,
1806-1873. Autobiography. 4. Mill, John Stuart,
1806-1873. Inaugural address at St. Andrews.
I. Title. II. Series: Landmarks in the history of
education.
[LB675.M5142C38 1979]   370.1   78-27822
ISBN 0-8371-4282-2

Published in 1931 by Cambridge University Press, London

Reprinted in 1979 by Greenwood Press, Inc.
51 Riverside Avenue, Westport, CT 06880

Printed in the United States of America

10 9 8 7 6 5 4 3 2 1

CONTENTS

INTRODUCTION

I

The early chapters of John Stuart Mill's *Autobiography* form the best introduction to a study of his father's views. For the system there described, though the most amazing ever devised by man, was of a piece with the Benthamite principle that, just as a nation's character is the result of its laws, so the individual character can by education be moulded to any pattern we please. "In psychology," says J. S. Mill of his father, "his fundamental doctrine was the formation of all human character by circumstances, through the universal Principle of Association, and the consequent unlimited possibility of improving the moral and intellectual condition of mankind by education. Of all his doctrines none was more important than this, or needs more to be insisted on; unfortunately there is none which is more contradictory to the prevailing tendencies of speculation, both in his time and since." As an educational doctrine this was not new. "I think I may say," writes Locke at the beginning of his *Thoughts concerning Education*, "that of all the men we meet with, nine parts of ten are what they are, good or evil, useful or not, by their education." Helvétius, James Mill's immediate master, exaggerates Locke's postulate of the *tabula rasa*: in his famous chapter "L'Education peut tout"[1] he asserts definitely that "l'éducation nous fait ce que nous sommes."

[1] Helvétius, *De l'Homme, de ses Facultés intellectuelles, et de son Education* (a posthumous work), sect. x, chap. i. The 4-volume edition of Helvétius' works (London, 1776) in the London Library was presented by J. S. Mill in April, 1841; one may guess that it came from his father's library.

Mill in his article on Education writes rather more cautiously. Just as Robert Owen claimed that "any character, from the best to the worst, from the most ignorant to the most enlightened, may be given *to any community*,"[1] so Mill claims that "This much, at any rate, is ascertained, that all the difference which exists, or can ever be made to exist, between one *class* of men, and another, is wholly owing to education."

In these contexts "education" is of course used in a wide sense; it means in fact "environment," or "nature" as we now distinguish it from "nurture." But even in the narrower sense of instruction, Mill deliberately set out to educate his son to a pattern; there was a concerted plan between him and Bentham to leave "the poor boy a successor worthy of both of us."[2] It is worth while inquiring how far the result bears out the theory that education can accomplish everything. We must first rid our minds of modern sentiments about childhood: it is irrelevant to say that Mill deserved prosecution for cruelty. Nor should we argue that both the Mills were people of abnormal ability; the question is whether John Mill became the sort of man that his father intended. In a sense he did: he undoubtedly carried on his father's work and succeeded him as leader of the Utilitarians; his very special training made him from an early age an acute thinker on logic and political economy. But while he retained many of the Benthamite principles, he changed Utilitarianism as a whole in a way that its originators would not have approved. And these changes arose from the developments in Mill's character which were directly opposed to his early education. Had he been the hard, unemotional, rather unpleasant man that his father was—even Bentham attributed his political opinions less to

[1] *New View of Society*, 1813.
[2] Hugh Elliot, Introduction to *Letters of John Stuart Mill*, p. xvi.

his love of the many than to his hatred of the few—all
would have gone according to plan; on the contrary, though
deficient on the sensual, he was more than commonly developed on the emotional side, as is amply proved by his
warm friendships and his infatuation for the lady whom he
eventually married.[1]

The turning point in Mill's development came, later
than with normal adolescents, at the age of twenty; it is
minutely described in the chapter "A Crisis in my Mental
History." After a long spell of overwork he fell into a
state of depression—a nervous breakdown, we should probably call it nowadays—in which he discovered that the
"advantage of a quarter of a century over his contemporaries" which his father's training had given him was of
no avail. His education had failed to create "the pleasure
of sympathy with human beings, and the feelings which
made the good of others, and especially of mankind on a
large scale, the object of existence." In other words, the
calculated pursuit of happiness, the foundation of Utilitarianism, had missed "the greatest and surest sources of
happiness." Further, he lacked what he calls "the passive
susceptibilities," the whole aesthetic side of life. Beauty
made no appeal to James Mill; "sentimentality" (as he
called anything poetical) was his bugbear; and so the whole
world of art, as having no connexion with political philosophy, was omitted from his son's training. Hence the
poetry of Wordsworth came as a divine revelation to Mill:
he had always felt the beauty of natural scenery; he now
found a new life in its transfiguration by the poet. Modern
psychology has emphasised almost *ad nauseam* the affective
side of human nature; but if there be any who still believe
in an exclusively rational education they should take warning

[1] *Ib.* Note on Mill's personal life, by Mary Taylor.

by John Stuart Mill. Had not nature triumphed over nurture he would either have lost his reason or at any rate have been unable to accomplish the noble work of his later life. Thus even for the specific end that James Mill had in view, to construct a Utilitarian robot, his system failed. Never has an education been more ably directed; it was a test case: education is not all-powerful.

Apart from this general question it is obvious that Mill's training overlooked other sides of human nature. It was entirely bookish: it "was in itself much more fitted for training me to *know* than to *do*." Again, in spite of the emphasis laid on physical education in James Mill's article, no room was left for play. His only exercise consisted of walks, during which he gave his father a summary of the books he had been reading. "I was never a boy," he said later, "never played at cricket; it is better to let Nature have her way."[1] With such a childhood, followed by a sedentary life, it is remarkable that he withstood so long the consumptive tendency of his family. One cannot even entirely agree that "whatever else it may have done" his education "proved how much more than is commonly supposed may be taught, and well taught, in those early years which, in the common modes of what is called instruction, are little better than wasted"; for this claim begs the question: it was this very saving of "waste" that did the damage.

So much for James Mill's educational practice. According to his own principles we shall expect to find his theory correspondingly erroneous; for he was rightly indignant at "the common expression that something was true in theory but required correction in practice." Yet it would be quite misleading to suggest that his article is without value; on the contrary it is one of the finest

[1] *Journals of Caroline Fox*, cit. Courtney, *Life of J. S. Mill*, p. 40.

treatises on education in the English language. Its interest is not merely historical, for Mill was in several ways a pioneer. Thus he definitely grounds educational theory on psychology: "the business is...to put the knowledge which we possess respecting the human mind, into that order and form, which is most advantageous for drawing from it the practical rules of education." We differ from him only that we now realise better the complexity of the human mind; we no longer suppose that it can be made "as plain as the road from Charing Cross to St Paul's."[1] Again, in his insistence on the influence of the body upon the mind, further knowledge has merely confirmed his speculations. It was the first attempt at a completely scientific treatment of education. Macaulay's jibes were not altogether un-provoked: Mill was in a way "an Aristotelian of the fifteenth century, born out of due season"; his style "is generally as dry as that of Euclid's Elements."[2] But in spite of all that, his close reasoning is well worth the effort of following; and a critical examination of his argument is highly instructive. Those who have studied none but modern psychology will learn much from his succinct account of the Associationist School, especially as its doc-trines die hard. And, as always, it is stimulating to study the working of a first-rate mind; for though James Mill's fame has been eclipsed by his son's, he was the more original and daring, possibly the more influential, thinker— a point on which John Stuart Mill, the most modest of men, had no illusions.

Regarding the article then as a treatise on educational theory, we are at once struck by certain imperfections. The most obvious has been well characterised by Bain;[3] it is

---

[1] Mill to Place, 6 Dec. 1817, cit. Halévy.
[2] "Mill on Government," *Edinburgh Rev.* March, 1829.
[3] Bain, *James Mill*, p. 247.

that "the *a priori*, or deductive handling is here exclusively carried out. The author hardly ever cites an actual experience in education; far less has he a body of experience summed up in empirical laws, to confront and compare with the deductions from the theory of the human mind. One would think he had never been either a learner or a teacher, so little does he avail himself of the facts or maxims of the work of the school." This is precisely the criticism with which Macaulay knocked the bottom out of Mill's article on Government: "We have here an elaborate treatise on Government, from which, but for two or three passing allusions, it would not appear that the author was aware that any governments actually existed among men. Certain propensities of human nature are assumed; and from these premises the whole science of politics is synthetically deduced." This attitude was of course typical of Bentham; it has been superseded by the historical method in political theory, just as in psychology it has been ousted by closer study of behaviour. Mill has in fact fallen into the very mistake, or its converse, that he warns us against. "To recommend the separation of practice from theory is, simply, to recommend bad practice"; he has, to adapt his own words, recommended bad theory. One would have thought that everyday observation would have destroyed Mill's belief (which was perpetuated by his son) in the natural equality of men, if it were not that the modern psychologists who pride themselves most on strict observation of objective fact, the Behaviorists, fall into the same error. "All healthy individuals," says John B. Watson,[1] "start out equal.... It is what happens to individuals after birth that makes one a hewer of wood and a drawer of water, another a diplomat, a thief, a successful business man or a far-famed scientist." No one can deny the partial truth of this statement: it

[1] *Behaviorism*, p. 217.

applies, however, only to the average person. Education cannot create the genius; it cannot create even the man of unusual ability. And it must always be conditioned by special aptitudes, as indeed was admitted by Helvétius himself. Speaking of training a boy to become a violinist he writes: "les progrès plus ou moins rapides de l'enfant dépendent ensuite de l'habilité du maître, de sa méthode meilleure ou moins bonne d'enseigner, *enfin du goût plus ou moins vif que l'élève prend pour son instrument.*"[1]

All this James Mill should have known very well from his experience as a private tutor, and from his active interest in the organisation of education. He was an early supporter of Lancaster, and took a violent part in the controversy against Dr Bell. The bitterness of that dispute is hard to understand now; but it may be gauged by the articles in the *Edinburgh* and *Quarterly*,[2] by James Mill's pamphlet *Schools for All* (1812), and Bentham's ponderous and unreadable *Church-of-Englandism* (1818). With Brougham, Place, and others, Mill formed the West London Lancasterian Association, the object of which was to organise a complete system of schools for London west of Temple Bar and north of the river. The scheme was not a success; but it led incidentally to another project, likewise unsuccessful—that of the Chrestomathic School. Intelligent men were then so impressed by the value of the "monitorial" or "mutual" system of instruction that they believed it capable of miraculous results.[3] Even a sensible man like Brougham writes: "It is manifest that any rule in algebra may be communicated by the same process" (i.e. by one ignorant boy reading the rules to another and making him

---

[1] *Op. cit.* sect. x, chap. vi.
[2] *Edinburgh*: Oct. 1806 (Sydney Smith), Oct. 1807, Nov. 1810, Nov. 1811 (Brougham), Feb. 1813 (James Mill). *Quarterly*: Oct. 1811 (Southey), Sept. 1812, July 1818.
[3] J. S. Mill knew better; see below, p. 80.

work examples mechanically) "from the simplest to the most intricate and refined—from the addition of two quantities to the methods of infinite series and fluents. Every part of geometrical science may be taught by similar means —from the first proposition in Euclid, to the sublime theories of Newton and Laplace.... In like manner, whatever branches of natural philosophy admit of a symbolical notation...are all capable of being communicated by a person ignorant of them, but able to read, to as many others as can hear the sound of his voice at once.... The method may, therefore, most truly be pronounced a capital discovery, in every point of view; and we have little doubt that it will speedily be extended from the sciences to the arts, which seem all to admit of being taught upon similar principles."[1] So it is not surprising that Mill, equally impressed, should have joined with Place in a plan for establishing a middle-class school—a secondary school as we should now call it—on Lancasterian lines. They managed to interest Bentham, who wrote a lengthy treatise, *Chrestomathia* (1816), containing a classification of all branches of knowledge; with it was bound up the "Proposal" (written by Mill and Place) "for erecting by Subscription, and carrying on by the name of the Chrestomathic School, a Day-School for the extension of the new system to the higher branches of Instruction and ranks in life." But subscriptions were slow in coming in; and Bentham, who had offered his garden as a site for the school, gradually withdrew; so the scheme failed to mature. Yet out of this Chrestomathic scheme, without its Lancasterian limitations, developed the most important of the diverse groups that united to found the University of London. The idea of the University was, of course, the poet Campbell's, but its carrying out was the work of more practical men. At

[1] *Edin. Rev.* Nov. 1810, p. 74.

INTRODUCTION

first, Place has recorded, Mill "discountenanced it, as he thought it was unattainable";[1] but he must soon have been convinced, for he became one of the most active workers.[2] The University was in full accord with Utilitarian ideas, of which Mill was then the recognised exponent; as Mr Bellot says, "the immediate source of Benthamite influence was not the master himself but his disciple James Mill."[3] The same influence led to the simultaneous foundation by Brougham of the Society for the Diffusion of Useful Knowledge,[4] which we may regard almost as the extramural department of the University. Its function was mainly the publication of cheap treatises on scientific subjects, at a low price, for the benefit of those who could not easily obtain a teacher. On the Committee of this Society Mill served from its start in 1827 until his death in 1836. Well might John Stuart Mill write that his father was "the good genius by the side of Brougham in most of what he did for the public, either on education, law reform, or any other subject."[5] Mill indeed had a strange admiration for Brougham: "it has always appeared to me a signal tribute to the intellectual eminence of the great orator, that the writer who, of all others, aimed most at terseness and perspicuity, should exhibit such deference to one whose reputation was built upon broader foundations than logical profundity or metaphysical subtility"—so writes Charles Knight[6] in his account of the Committee members. But

[1] Bain, *op. cit.* p. 262.
[2] He was a member of the first Council, and convener of the Education Committee. One characteristic detail is that he secured the appointment of the Rev. John Hoppus, who for thirty years incompetently held the chair of Philosophy, because he professed to follow Hartley.
[3] Bellot, *University College, London*, p. 25.
[4] See *Journal of Adult Education*, Oct. 1929.
[5] *Autobiog.* chap. iv.
[6] *Passages of a Working Life*, II, 119.

b-2

Mill's admiration is more strikingly expressed in a letter to Brougham (28 Dec. 1833): "I hope you duly consider one duty, the care of your health. I know not when the time was, in the history of our species, that more depended on the health of one man, than depends at this moment on yours. The progress of mankind would lose a century by the loss of you. Think what that is."[1] This is the typical respect of the thinker for the man of action; but it is plain that for the many good services done by Brougham to the cause of education, James Mill was very largely responsible. Hence the wrongheadedness of his theory is all the more surprising.

If we ask how so clear-sighted a man as James Mill should have made this mistake, the answer seems to be that his theory was a "rationalisation" of his desire to see society transformed by education. For this possibility he found support in the mechanistic psychology of Hartley and Helvétius, a psychology which he amplified and systematised in his *Analysis of the Human Mind* (1829). Mill indeed provided the Utilitarian philosophy with an adequate psychology. His own development is interesting. Trained at Edinburgh, he was immensely impressed by the eloquence of Dugald Stewart and for some years remained an adherent of the Scottish school of Intuitionism. But under the influence of Bentham he was completely converted to the Associationist theory, which he expounds in this article on Education and the *Analysis*. The two theories differed fundamentally in their way of explaining the acquisition of knowledge. The school represented by Hartley followed Locke (forgetting his other principle, Reflection) in attributing all knowledge to sensation; the whole mental life accordingly is for them built up by the associations ("sequences" or "trains," as Mill calls them) which come about by accident or

[1] Bain, *op. cit.* p. 371.

by the design of the educator. Their opponents, represented by Kant and by the Scottish school, believed in "original feelings" or intuitions which are not derived from sensation. The question, as Mill points out (p. 8), is of the first importance for education; for, if Hartley is right, by manipulating our pupil's experience—by a skilful choice of "conditioned reflexes," to adopt the Behaviorist jargon—we can control his entire development. We do not yet fully understand the relations between heredity and environment; but we should not nowadays find much agreement with those who entirely neglect either factor. The solution, so far as one has been reached, lies in a synthesis of the two; it is familiar to modern students in the doctrine of Sir Percy Nunn, "that the living organism has a principle of autonomy, of self-determination, which does not, indeed, make it independent of endowment and environment, but does enable it to give its own characteristic form to, and make its own original use of, what it derives from those sources."[1] But for the pre-evolutionary mind of James Mill such a conception would have been impossible; he had formed a perfectly clear and consistent philosophy of education, which in his day it would have been hard to demolish.

However, as Mill says (p. 29), more important than the answer to this general question is the determination of the "efficient practical rules" which emerge from psychology. Since mental life depends entirely on associations (sequences) it is essential to provide those that will result in right habits; their effects will be stamped in by Pleasure and Pain (another tenet of the Utilitarians). The ultimate end of education is happiness; but Mill has the honesty to admit that the nature of happiness is not yet determined. But he is quite certain about the "desirable qualities of the

[1] *Education: its Data and First Principles*, p. 118.

human mind" requisite to attain happiness: these affect
either the individual or society.   Of the first class he
specifies (1) Intelligence, which includes Knowledge and
Sagacity, (2) Temperance, or the control of appetites (when
it takes the form of resisting pain he calls it Fortitude). The
social qualities are (1) Justice, which means doing no harm
to others and (2) Generosity, which means doing good to
others. Mill in fact finds that the four cardinal virtues of
the ancients can be adopted with little change. It is characteristic of Mill that Knowledge should take the first place
among the aims of education, as with Dr Arnold it took
the last; we may contrast also Mr Bertrand Russell's
list: vitality, courage, sensitiveness, and intelligence. The
modern psychologist would object to the inclusion of knowledge as a constituent of intelligence; yet no intelligence
test can be framed which does not require knowledge of
some kind for its solution: the most we can do is to exclude
knowledge that is likely to be acquired at school. But Mill
certainly forestalls (though for different reasons) the
Freudian emphasis on the importance attaching to the
earliest impressions. In one of his first writings there occurs
a passage so true and so modern in spirit that it is worth
quoting at length. Reviewing a book by one Millar, he
writes:

"It appears to us that few biographers have the same
opinions which we have formed respecting the importance
of the early part of life. When a man has risen to great
intellectual or moral eminence, the process by which his
mind was formed is one of the most instructive circumstances which can be unveiled to mankind.

"It displays to their view the means of acquiring excellence, and suggests the most persuasive motive to employ
them. When, however, we are merely told that a man went
to such a school on such a day, and such a college on

another, our curiosity may be somewhat gratified, but we have received no lesson. We know not the discipline to which his own will, and the recommendation of his teachers subjected him. We may conclude that young Millar studied hard, from the effects which afterwards appeared. But we are not introduced to the particulars of his studies. We have no hint with regard to the circumstances which kindled his ardour, or those by which the flame was fed. This is the matter of primary importance in the life of any man. To this is owing whatever excellence he may discover in the labours of Science, or the active business of mankind. With regard to this important particular much more might we think be discovered by those who write the lives of eminent men, near the time when they flourished, than we generally find. At any rate, in whatever obscurity the causes of their ardour might remain, the degree of it which they exhibited in early life might in most cases be pretty accurately described, as well as the direction in which it impelled them. We might learn the studies in which they delighted, the books which they chiefly perused, the hours which they were accustomed to give to labour, and those which they resigned to relaxation; even the nature of the sports in which they indulged, might be a circumstance frequently not unworthy of regard.

"The people among whom an eminent man spent the days of childhood and youth; the character of his parents and teachers; and the style of behaviour which they manifested towards him, ought always to be an object of peculiar attention. Our biographers, like our historians, aiming only at the magnificent, seem to think that the occupations and character of the schoolboy are altogether below their notice. But if the business of education be of that importance which we suppose, their mistake is egregious. If too our knowledge with regard to education, our knowledge of the means by which intellectual and moral excellence may be communicated, is so imperfect, of what consequence should it not be deemed, to obtain the most minute information with regard to the means actually employed in producing those instances of great talents and virtues which have really appeared?"[1]

Contemporary biographers, notably M. Maurois, are well aware of this truth.

The section on physical education is interesting, not so much intrinsically, for most of its details are obsolete, but as marking a real attempt to define the relations between body and mind. In quite recent years the science of psychopathology has grown up; we have learnt something of the effects of the endocrine glands, and of vitamins; we are beginning, through the researches of industrial psychology, to understand the conditions of efficient labour. But Mill, with knowledge that he realised to be inadequate, saw clearly the importance of the bodily side. "It follows," he writes in an eloquent passage, "that when we deliberate about the means of introducing intellectual and moral excellence, into the minds of the principal portion of the people, one of the first things which we are bound to provide for, is, a generous and animating diet. The physical causes must go along with the moral; and nature herself forbids, that you shall make a wise and virtuous people, out of a starving one.... Though far from fond of paradoxical expressions, we are tempted to say, that a good diet is a necessary part of a good education; for in one very important sense it is emphatically true. In the great body of the people all education is impotent without it." Such words contain no paradox to modern ears: the School Medical Service was started with the hope of improving a "C 3 nation"; yet until there are fewer slums and more

[1] From a review in the *Literary Journal*, 1806. Cit. Bain, p. 56.

playing fields the ideal is far from realisation. Even now 40 per cent. of children enter the elementary schools in a state of disease, mostly preventible.

The remainder of the article consists of a detailed application of the "desirable qualities," Intelligence, Temperance, Justice, and Generosity, to the four main types of education, which he names Domestic, Technical, Social, and Political. Mill constantly apologises for the sketchy treatment: one must remember that he was writing an encyclopaedia article. There is no discussion of the subjects to be included in the curriculum or of teaching methods, though we know from his son's *Autobiography* that he had decided opinions upon both questions. He is concerned rather with the aims of the various departments of education, and with their effects on the individual and on society, —for (as one would expect from a Utilitarian) the "great object of desire" is that each should fit himself to be and actually become "the instrument of the greatest possible benefit to his fellow men." Hence the means should not be pains and terror, the common and easy means of bad education: it is not thus that happiness will be secured. The language may be old-fashioned and pedantic, but it expresses a truth as important to-day as when it was written. Further, Mill is very modern in his desire to see the field of education widened. He lived in a day when "the schoolmaster was abroad," when widespread if muddled efforts to provide popular education on a large scale were being made. But whilst these efforts were based on restricted motives, Mill took the noble view that "the question, whether the people should be educated, is the same with the question, whether they should be happy or miserable."[1] Even though

[1] But he did not reach the truth enunciated by Herbert Spencer: "the usual test of political legislation—its tendency to promote happiness—is beginning to be, in a great degree, the test of legislation in the school and the nursery."

a large number must, from the economic necessities of life, be precluded from continued study, yet "we have no doubt that it will appear that a very high degree is attainable by them," especially if they are allowed a longer period of schooling in youth. Mill evidently had a clear vision of the possibilities of adult education, which he helped Birkbeck and Brougham to work out—as he helped also to bring into being the kind of university that he sketches, freed from "old practices which have become a hackneyed routine."

Thus though Mill's theory, as embodied in the education of his son, was neither successful nor sound, his educational policy for the nation foreshadowed much that has since come about. His was a stern and limited nature; but he had a genuine will to improve the world. The Utilitarian philosophy provided a panacea; and the initial step towards carrying it out lay in education. If education has not proved quite so powerful as he supposed, at least it has accomplished much. We are coming back to the wide interpretation which he gave to the word; and as our schools become less exclusively bookish, as the "action of the political machine" more effectively determines "the state of the aliment and labour of the lower classes," it may turn out to be true that "if education does not perform everything, there is hardly anything which it does not perform."

II

The office of Rector of St Andrews University is a survival from the mediaeval student-university, in which the student body was governed by its own elected officer. In modern times the duties are mainly ornamental. The Rector is officially President of the Court; and he is expected to visit the University when he can and to deliver one or more addresses to the students. To this office Mill was elected, without his permission, in 1865; he would have liked to withdraw, but compromised by arranging to defer his inaugural address till 1867. Mill has had many distinguished successors[1]—Froude, Dean Stanley, Lord Balfour, Lord Rosebery, Barrie, Kipling, and Nansen, to mention but a few—but none can have given so overpowering an inaugural address; its delivery, Bain[2] tells us, lasted three hours. "Its absolute value is considerable; but in relation to the time, place, and circumstances, I consider it to have been a mistake.... The performance was a failure, in my opinion, for this simple reason, that he had no conception of the limits of a University curriculum." Its length need not deter readers who have not to listen for three hours to Mill's thin high-pitched voice; and though the course of study that he sketches out is plainly beyond the powers of a university student—like Milton's, "this is not a bow for every man to shoot in that counts himself a teacher"—yet we may gain much from his broad treatment of higher education.

Like his father he distinguishes the narrower from the wider sense of education; but even this is sufficiently wide: "the culture which each generation purposely gives to those who are to be its successors, in order to qualify them for at least keeping up, and if possible for raising, the level of improvement which has been attained." It is a noble, if not very practicable, conception. The general aim of the Address is "to pass in review every essential department of general culture...to offer a few remarks on each of those departments, considered in its relation to human cultivation at large: adverting to the nature of the claims which each has to a place in liberal education; in what special

[1] The office, and an honorary degree, were characteristically declined by Herbert Spencer (1871); see his *Autobiog.* II, p. 232.
[2] Bain, *John Stuart Mill*, p. 126.

manner they each conduce to the improvement of the individual mind and the benefit of the race; and how they all conspire to the common end, the strengthening, exalting, purifying, and beautifying of our common nature, and the fitting out of mankind with the necessary mental implements for the work they have to perform through life."

In several details Mill's attitude bears marks of his own education. His somewhat exaggerated advocacy of a classical foundation, coupled with his scorn for the time wasted by bad teaching, recall his father's Greek lessons at the age of three. He himself learned French during his stay with Sir Samuel Bentham in France, and realised the economy of picking up a foreign language by living in the country. "Who ever really learned history and geography except by private reading?" he asks; he certainly so acquired them himself; but the rule could not apply to many—and as geography is now understood, perhaps to none. Again, in pressing the early study of ecclesiastical history and of logic he assumes that what was good for him would suit others. These however are comparatively unimportant points; and on some of them he might think differently were he now alive. Thus his defence of the classics was undoubtedly a counterblast to the recent attack by Herbert Spencer; and he would doubtless write less superficially about science if he knew of its modern developments. The fact is that, as Spencer[1] pointed out, Mill and the Utilitarians generally lacked discipline in physical science; as in political and moral theory and in psychology they were

---

[1] Spencer, *op. cit.* II, 89. He says that Mill in this Address "urged the claims of Classics, with the apparent implication that they were in danger of being over-ridden by Science. Considering that Science was but just beginning to raise its head, and to obtain a grudging recognition in the high places of learning, it seemed to me that the note of alarm was scarcely called for." *Ib.* p. 156; see also p. 122.

content with *a priori* speculations, so in physical science
they had not made that study "which conduces to an ever-
present and vivid consciousness of cause."

A more serious defect is Mill's adherence to the doctrine
of "formal training." On this difficult subject psychology
has not altogether made up its mind. We know at any rate
that the transfer from one subject of study to another is
slight, and that all we can hope for is the formation of
certain sentiments and habits of mind; further, that such
habits will result more surely from diversified than from
very specialised study. So much Mill seems to have recognised; "experience proves that there is no one study or
pursuit, which, practised to the exclusion of all others, does
not narrow and pervert the mind"; and again, "even
trained minds, when all their training is on a special subject,
and does not extend to the general principles of induction,
are only kept right when there are ready opportunities of
verifying their inferences by fact." It is such a habit of
mind that Mill means when he says that "familiarity with
scientific experiment at least does the useful service of inspiring a wholesome scepticism about the conclusions which
the mere surface of experience suggests"; in this remark we
can agree with him, except for the implication, which runs
through the whole Address, that any course of training will
necessarily have more general effects. "If there were no
more to be said than that scientific education teaches us to
think, and literary education to express our thoughts, do
we not require both?" The conclusion is justified, but not
the grounds on which it is based. It is strange that he
should thus have confined discipline in thought to science,
when a few pages later he attributes the most scientific type
of thought ("to question all things; never to turn away
from any difficulty, etc.") to a study of the ancient dialecticians. He is equally wrong in his remarks about evidence:

"the models of the art of estimating evidence are furnished
by science; the rules are suggested by science; and the study
of science is the most fundamental portion of the practice"
—for he neglects the obvious ambiguity of the word
"evidence." We are still on dangerous ground when we
discuss formal training; and Mill was probably as clear
about it as was possible in his day. The mass of subsequent
experimentation has partially cleared, but partially ob-
scured, the issue.

The most valuable parts of the Address are those in
which he deals with general and specific knowledge, and
with logic. His warnings on the evils arising from too
specialised knowledge are even more needed in these days
of constantly increasing specialisation. This tendency is
due in part to the enormous mass of knowledge that has
grown up around every subject; but it has been so accen-
tuated by examinations, particularly those for the Higher
Certificate and for Honours degrees, that a radical change
is generally felt to be necessary. Where Mill is genuinely
helpful is in his distinction between "a general and a superficial knowledge": what he advocates is no smattering, but
a knowledge of general principles, and of the authorities to
consult. It may be quite impossible for one ignorant of
mathematics to understand modern physics; but that is no
excuse for leaving the subject entirely alone. We must
however remember his caution to "mark well the dividing
line between what we know accurately and what we do
not," and his equally useful remark "that it is idle to throw
away time upon the details of anything which is to form
no part of the occupation of our practical energies." But it
must be admitted that the famous maxim, to know something of everything and everything of something, puts the
whole matter in a more cogent form; Mill's gifts did not
include epigram.

In Mill's age the meaning of a liberal education was frequently discussed.[1] Herbert Spencer's *Education* was published in 1861; Newman's lectures, collected as *The Idea of a University*, were delivered in 1852; Huxley's address, "A Liberal Education; and where to find it," was given in 1868; and in the year of Mill's address, 1867, there appeared a notable volume of *Essays on a Liberal Education*, edited by F. W. Farrar, then an assistant master at Harrow. There is no more illuminating study for the student of education than a careful comparison of these Victorian essays with more modern conceptions, such as those of Sir Michael Sadler and Professor Whitehead. Each generation necessarily has its own philosophy of education, but can gain from an understanding of the past. Mill's contribution cannot rank with the greatest, but it is a sincere and attractive exposition of a worthy ideal.

[1] The Clarendon Commission had reported on the Public Schools in 1864; the Schools Inquiry Commission under Lord Taunton was still sitting. The Royal Commissions on Oxford and Cambridge had done their work in the early fifties.

I

JAMES MILL'S ARTICLE ON EDUCATION

Introduction.—Extent of the Subject.—The
different Questions which it involves.

The end of Education is to render the individual, as much
as possible, an instrument of happiness, first to himself, and
next to other beings.

The properties, by which he is fitted to become an instrument to this end, are, partly, those of the body, and
partly those of the mind.

Happiness depends upon the condition of the body, either
immediately, as where the bodily powers are exerted for the
attainment of some good; or mediately, through the mind,
as where the condition of the body affects the qualities of
the mind.

Education, in the sense in which it is usually taken, and
in which it shall here be used, denotes the means which
may be employed to render the *mind*, as far as possible, an
operative cause of happiness. The mode in which the *body*
may be rendered the most fit for operating as an instrument
of happiness is generally considered as a different species of
inquiry; belonging to physicians, and others, who study the
means of perfecting the bodily powers.

Education, then, in the sense in which we are now using
the term, may be defined, the best employment of all the
means which can be made use of, by man, for rendering
the human mind to the greatest possible degree the cause of
human happiness. Every thing, therefore, which operates,
from the first germ of existence, to the final extinction of

life, in such a manner as to affect those qualities of the mind on which happiness in any degree depends, comes within the scope of the present inquiry. Not to turn every thing to account is here, if any where, bad economy, in the most emphatical sense of the phrase.

The field, it will easily be seen, is exceedingly comprehensive. It is everywhere, among enlightened men, a subject of the deepest complaint, that the business of education is ill performed; and that, in this, which might have been supposed the most interesting of all human concerns, the practical proceedings are far from corresponding with the progress of the human mind. It may be remarked, that, notwithstanding all that has been written on the subject, even the *theory* of education has not kept pace with philosophy; and it is unhappily true, that the *practice* remains to a prodigious distance behind the theory. One reason why the theory, or the combination of ideas which the present state of knowledge might afford for improving the business of education, remains so imperfect, probably is, that the writers have taken but a partial view of the subject; in other words, the greater number have mistaken a part of it for the whole. And another reason of not less importance is, that they have generally contented themselves with vague ideas of the object or end to which education is required as the means. One grand purpose of the present inquiry will be to obviate all those mistakes; and, if not to exhibit that comprehensive view, which we think is desirable, but to which our limits are wholly inadequate; at any rate, to conduct the reader into that train of thought which will lead him to observe for himself the boundaries of the subject. If a more accurate conception is formed of the end, a better estimate will be made of what is suitable as the means.

1. It has been remarked, that every thing, from the first germ of existence to the final extinction of life, which

operates in such a manner as to affect those qualities of the mind on which happiness in any degree depends, comes within the scope of the present inquiry. Those circumstances may be all arranged, according to the hackneyed division, under two heads: They are either physical or moral; meaning by physical, those of a material nature, which operate more immediately upon the material part of the frame; by moral, those of a mental nature, which operate more immediately upon the mental part of the frame.

2. In order to know in what manner things operate upon the mind, it is necessary to know how the mind is constructed. *Quicquid recipitur, recipitur ad modum recipientis.* This is the old aphorism, and nowhere more applicable than to the present case. If you attempt to act upon the mind, in ways not adapted to its nature, the least evil you incur is to lose your labour.

3. As happiness is the end, and the means ought to be nicely adapted to the end, it is necessary to inquire, What are the qualities of mind which chiefly conduce to happiness,—both the happiness of the individual himself, and the happiness of his fellow-creatures?

It appears to us, that this distribution includes the whole of the subject. Each of these divisions branches itself out into a great number of inquiries. And, it is manifest, that the complete developement of any one of them would require a greater space than we can allow for the whole. It is, therefore, necessary for us, if we aim at a comprehensive view, to confine ourselves to a skeleton.

The first of these inquiries is the most practical, and, therefore, likely to be the most interesting. Under the Physical Head, it investigates the mode in which the qualities of the mind are affected by the health, the aliment, the air, the labour, &c. to which the individual is subject.

Under the Moral Head it includes what may be called, 1. Domestic Education, or the mode in which the mind of the individual is liable to be formed by the conduct of the individuals composing the family in which he is born and bred: 2. Technical or scholastic education, including all those exercises upon which the individual is put, as means to the acquisition of habits,—habits either conducive to intellectual and moral 'excellence, or even to the practice of the manual arts: 3. Social education, or the mode in which the mind of the individual is acted upon by the nature of the political institutions under which he lives.

The two latter divisions comprehend what is more purely theoretical; and the discussion of them offers fewer attractions to that class of readers, unhappily numerous, to whom intellectual exercises have not by habit been rendered delightful. The inquiries, however, which are included under these divisions, are required as a foundation to those included under the first. The fact is, that good practice can, in no case, have any solid foundation but in sound theory. This proposition is not more important, than it is certain. For, What is theory? The *whole* of the knowledge, which we possess upon any subject, put into that order and form in which it is most easy to draw from it good practical rules. Let any one examine this definition, article by article, and show us that it fails in a single particular. To recommend the separation of practice from theory is, therefore, simply, to recommend bad practice.

SECTION I

Theory of the Human Mind.—Its Importance in the Doctrine of Education.

1. The first, then, of the inquiries, embraced by the great subject of education, is that which regards the nature of the human mind; and the business is, agreeably to the foregoing definition of theory, to put the knowledge which we possess respecting the human mind, into that order and form, which is most advantageous for drawing from it the practical rules of education. The question is, How the mind, with those properties which it possesses, can, through the operation of certain means, be rendered most conducive to a certain end? To answer this question, the whole of its properties must be known. The whole science of human nature is, therefore, but a branch of the science of education. Nor can education assume its most perfect form, till the science of the human mind has reached its highest point of improvement. Even an outline, however, of the philosophy of the human mind would exceed the bounds of the present article; we must, therefore, show what ought to be done, rather than attempt, in any degree, to execute so extensive a project.

With respect to the human mind, as with respect to every thing else, all that passes with us under the name of knowledge is either matter of experience, or, to carry on the analogy of expression, matter of guess. The first is real knowledge; the properties of the object correspond to it. The latter is supposititious knowledge, and the properties of the object do or do not correspond to it; most likely not. The first thing desirable is, to make an exact separation of those two kinds of knowledge; and, as much as possible, to confine ourselves to the first.

What, then, is it which we experience with regard to

the human mind? And what is it which we guess? We have experience of ourselves, when we *see*, when we *hear*, when we *taste*, when we *imagine*, when we *fear*, when we *love*, when we *desire*; and so on. And we give names, as above, to distinguish what we experience of ourselves, on one of those occasions, from what we experience on another. We have experience of other men exhibiting *signs* of having similar experiences of themselves, that is, of *seeing, hearing*, and so on. It is necessary to explain, shortly, what is here meant by a sign. When we ourselves *see, hear, imagine*, &c. certain actions of ours commonly follow. We know, accordingly, that if any one, observing those actions, were to infer that we had been *seeing, hearing*, &c. the inference would be just. As often then as we observe similar actions in other men, we infer that they, too, have been seeing or hearing; and we thus regard the action as the sign.

Having got names to distinguish the state or experience of ourselves, when we say, *I see, I hear, I wish*, and so on; we find occasion for a name which will distinguish the having any (be it what it may) of those experiences, from the being altogether without them; and, for this purpose, we say, *I feel*, which will apply, generally, to any of the cases in which we say, *I see*, or *hear*, or *remember*, or *fear*; and comprehends the meaning of them all. The term *I think*, is commonly used for a purpose nearly the same. But it is not quite so comprehensive: there are several things which we should include under the term *our experience of our mind*, to which we should not extend the term *I think*. But there is nothing included under it to which we should not extend the term *I feel*. This is truly, therefore, the generic term.

All our experience, then, of the human mind, is confined to the several occasions on which the term *I feel* can be applied. And, now, What does all this experience amount to? What is the knowledge which it affords? It is, first, a knowledge of the *feelings* themselves; we can remember what, one by one, they were. It is, next, a knowledge of the order in which they follow one another; and this is all. But this description, though a just one, is so very general as to be little instructive. It is not easy, however, to speak about those feelings minutely and correctly; because the language which we must apply to them, is ill adapted to the purpose.

Let us advert to the first branch of this knowledge, that of the feelings themselves. The knowledge of the simple cases, may be regarded as easy; the feeling is distinct at the moment of experience, and is distinctly remembered afterwards. But the difficulty is great with the complex cases. It is found, that a great number of simple feelings are apt to become so closely united, as often to assume the appearance of only one feeling, and to render it extremely difficult to distinguish from one another the simple feelings of which it is composed. And one of the grand questions which divide the philosophers of the present day, is, which feelings are simple, and which are complex. There are two sorts which all have regarded as simple: those which we have when we say, I hear, I see, I feel, I taste, I smell, corresponding to the five senses, and the copies of these sensations, called ideas of sense. Of these, the second take place only in consequence of the first, they are, as it were, a revival of them; not the same feelings with the sensations or impressions on the senses, but feelings which bear a certain resemblance to them. Thus, when a man sees the light of noon, the feeling he has is called an *impression*,— the impression of light; when he shuts his eyes and has a feeling,—the type or relict of the impression,—he is not said to *see* the light, or to have the *impression* of light, but to *conceive* the light, or have an idea of it.

These two,—*impressions*, and their corresponding *ideas*, —are simple feelings, in the opinion of all philosophers. But there is one set of philosophers who think that these are the only simple feelings, and that all the rest are merely combinations of them. There is another class of philosophers who think that there are original feelings beside impressions and ideas; as those which correspond to the words *remember, believe, judge, space, time, &c.* Of the first are Hartley and his followers in England, Condillac and his followers in France; of the second description are Dr. Reid and his followers in this country, Kant and the German school of metaphysicians in general on the Continent.

It is evident, that the determination of this question with regard to the first branch of enquiry, namely, what the feelings are, is of very great importance with regard to the second branch, namely, what is the order in which those feelings succeed one another. For how can it be known how they succeed one another, if we are ignorant which of them enter into those several groups which form the component parts of the train? It is of vast importance, then, for the business of education, that the analysis of mind should be accurately performed; in other words, that all our complex feelings should be accurately resolved into the simple ones of which they are composed. This, too, is of absolute necessity for the accurate use of language; as the greater number of words are employed to denote those groups of simple feelings which we call complex ideas.

In regard to all events, relating to mind or body, our knowledge extends not beyond two points: The first is, a knowledge of the events themselves; the second is, a knowledge of the order of their succession. The expression in words of the first kind of knowledge is history; the expression of the second is philosophy; and to render that expression short and clear is the ultimate aim of philosophy.

The first steps in ascertaining the order of succession among events are familiar and easy. One occurs, and then another, and after that a third, and so on; but at first it is uncertain whether this order is not merely accidental, and such as may never recur. After a time it is observed, that events, similar to those which have already occurred, are occurring again and again. It is next observed, that they are always followed, too, by the same sort of events by which those events were followed to which they are similar; that these second events are followed, in the third place, by events exactly similar to those which followed the events which they resemble; and that there is, thus, an endless round of the same sequences.

If the order in which one event follows another were always different, we should know events only one by one, and they would be infinitely too numerous to receive names. If we could observe none but very short sequences, if, for example, we could ascertain that one event was, indeed, always followed by one other of the same description, but could not trace any constancy farther, we should thus know events by sequences of twos and twos. But those sequences would also be a great deal too numerous to receive names.

The history of the human mind informs us, that the sequences which are first observed are short ones. They are still, therefore, too numerous to receive names. But men compound the matter. They give names to sequences which they are most interested in observing, and leave the rest unnamed. When they have occasion to speak of the un-named successions, they apply to them, the best way they can, the names which they have got; endeavouring to make a partial naming answer an universal purpose. And hence almost all the confusion of language and of thought arises.

The great object, then, is, to ascertain sequences more and more extensive, till, at last, the succession of all events may be reduced to a number of sequences sufficiently small for each of them to receive a name; then, and then only, shall we be able to speak wholly free from confusion.

Language affords an instructive example of this mode of ascertaining sequences. In language, the words are the events. When an ignorant man first hears another speak an unknown language, he hears the sounds one by one, but observes no sequence. At last he gathers a knowledge of the use of a few words, and then he has observed a few sequences; and so he goes on till he understands whatever he hears. The sequences, however, which he has observed, are of no greater extent than is necessary to understand the meaning of the speaker; they are, by consequence, very numerous and confusing.

Next comes the grammarian; and he, by dividing the words into different kinds, observes that these kinds follow one another in a certain order, and thus ascertains more enlarged sequences, which, by consequence, reduces their number.

Nor is this all; it is afterwards observed, that words consist, some of one syllable, and some of more than one; that all language may thus be resolved into syllables, and that syllables are much less in number than words; that, therefore, the number of sequences in which they can be formed are less in number, and, by consequence, are more extensive. This is another step in tracing to the most comprehensive sequences the order of succession in that class of events wherein language consists.

It is afterwards observed, that these syllables themselves are compounded; and it is at last found, that they may all be resolved into a small number of elementary sounds corresponding to the simple letters. All language is then found to consist of a limited number of sequences, made up of the different combinations of a few letters.

It is not pretended that the example of language is exactly parallel to the case which it is brought to illustrate. It is sufficient if it aids the reader in seizing the idea which we mean to convey. It shews the analogy between the analysing of a complex sound, namely, a word, into the simple sounds of which it is composed, to wit, letters; and the analysing of a complex feeling, such as the idea of a rose, into the simple feelings of sight, of touch, of taste, of smell, of which the complex idea or feeling is made up. It affords, also, a proof of the commanding knowledge which is attained of a train of events, by observing the sequences which are formed of the simplest elements into which they can be resolved; and it thus illustrates the two grand operations, by successful perseverance in which the knowledge of the human mind is to be perfected.

It is upon a knowledge of the sequences which take place in the human feelings or thoughts, that the structure of education must be reared. And, though much undoubtedly remains to be cleared up, enough is already known of those sequences to manifest the shameful defects of that education with which our supineness, and love of things as they are, rest perfectly satisfied.

As the happiness, which is the end of education, depends upon the actions of the individual, and as all the actions of man are produced by his feelings or thoughts, the business of education is, to make certain feelings or thoughts take place instead of others. The business of education, then, is to work upon the mental successions. As the sequences among the letters or simple elements of speech, may be made to assume all the differences between nonsense and the most sublime philosophy, so the sequences, in the feelings which constitute human thought, may assume all the differences between the extreme of madness and of wickedness, and the greatest attainable heights of wisdom and virtue: And almost the whole of this is the effect of education. That, at least, all the difference which exists between classes or bodies of men is the effect of education, will, we suppose, without entering into the dispute about individual distinctions, be readily granted; that it is education wholly which constitutes the remarkable difference between the Turk and the Englishman, and even the still more remarkable difference between the most cultivated European and the wildest savage. Whatever is made of any *class* of men, we may then be sure is possible to be made of the whole human race. What a field for exertion! What a prize to be won!

Mr. Hobbs, who saw so much further into the texture of human thought than all who had gone before him, was the first man, as far as we remember, who pointed out (what is peculiarly *knowledge* in this respect) the order in which our feelings succeed one another, as a distinct object of study. He marked, with sufficient clearness, the existence, and the cause of the sequences; but, after a very slight attempt to trace them, he diverged to other inquiries, which had this but indirectly for their object.

"The succession," he says (*Human Nature*, ch. 4.) "of conceptions, in the mind, series or consequence" (by *consequence* he means *sequence*) "of one after another, may be casual and incoherent, as in dreams, for the most part; and it may be orderly, as when the former thought introduceth the latter. The cause of the coherence or consequence (*sequence*) of one conception to another, is their first coherence or consequence at that time when they are produced by sense; as, for example, from St. Andrew the mind runneth to St. Peter, because their names are read together; from St. Peter to a stone, for the same cause; from stone to foundation, because we see them together; and, according to this example, the mind may run almost from any thing to any thing. But, as in the sense, the conception of cause and effect may succeed one another, so may they, *after* sense, in the imagination." By the succession in the *imagination* it is evident he means the succession of *ideas*, as by the succession in *sense* he means the succession of sensations.

Having said that the conceptions of *cause* and *effect* may succeed one another in the sense, and after sense in the imagination, he adds, "And, for the most part, they do so; the cause whereof is the appetite of them who, having a conception of the *end*, have next unto it a conception of the next *means* to that end; as when a man from a thought of honour, to which he hath an appetite, cometh to the thought of wisdom, which is the next means thereunto; and from thence to the thought of study, which is the next means to wisdom." (Ib.) Here is a declaration with respect to three grand laws in the sequence of our thoughts. The first is, that the succession of ideas follows the same order which takes place in that of the impressions. The second is, that the order of cause and effect is the most common order in the successions in the imagination, that is, in the succession of ideas. And the third is, that the appetites of individuals have a great power over the successions of ideas; as the thought of the object which the individual desires, leads him to the thought of that by which he may attain it.

Mr. Locke took notice of the sequence in the train of ideas, or the order in which they follow one another, only for a particular purpose;—to explain the intellectual singularities which distinguish particular men. "Some of our ideas," he says, "have a natural correspondence and connection one with another. It is the office and excellence of our reason to trace these, and hold them together in that union and correspondence which is founded in their peculiar beings. Besides this, there is another connexion of ideas,

wholly owing to chance or custom; ideas that are not at
all of kin come to be so united in some men's minds, that
it is very hard to separate them; they always keep in company, and the one no sooner at any time comes into the
understanding, but its associate appears with it; and if they
are more than two which are thus united, the whole gang,
always inseparable, show themselves together." There is
no attempt here to trace the order of sequence, or to ascertain which antecedents are followed by which consequents;
and the accidental, rather than the more general phenomena, are those which seem particularly to have struck his
attention. He gave, however, a name to the matter of fact.
When one idea is regularly followed by another, he called
this constancy of conjunction *the association of the ideas*;
and this is the name by which, since the time of Locke, it
has been commonly distinguished.

Mr. Hume perceived much more distinctly than any of
the philosophers who had gone before him, that to philo-
sophize concerning the human mind, was to trace the order
of succession among the elementary feelings of the man.
He pointed out three great laws or comprehensive sequences, which he thought included the whole. Ideas
followed one another, he said, according to *resemblance*,
contiguity in time and place, and *cause and effect*. The last
of these, the sequence according to cause and effect, was
very distinctly conceived, and even the cause of it explained
by Mr. Hobbs. That of contiguity in time and place is thus
satisfactorily explained by Mr. Hume. "It is evident," he
says, "that as the senses, in changing their objects, are
necessitated to change them regularly, and take them as
they lie contiguous to each other, the imagination must, by
long custom, acquire the same method of thinking, and run
along the parts of space and time in conceiving its objects."
(*Treatise of Human Nature*, P. 1. B. 1. sect. 4.) This is a

reference to one of the laws pointed out by Hobbs, namely, that the order of succession among the ideas, follows the order that took place among the impressions. Mr. Hume shows, that the order of sense is much governed by contiguity, and why; and assigns this as a sufficient reason of the order which takes place in the imagination. Of the next sequence, that according to resemblance, he gives no account, and only appeals to the consciousness of his reader for the existence of the fact. Mr. Hume farther remarked, that what are called our complex ideas, are only a particular class of cases belonging to the same law—the law of the succession of ideas; every complex idea being only a certain number of simple ideas, which succeed each other so rapidly, as not to be separately distinguished without an effort of thought. This was a great discovery; but it must at the same time be owned, that it was very imperfectly developed by Mr. Hume. That philosopher proceeded, by aid of these principles, to account for the various phenomena of the human mind. But though he made some brilliant developements, it is nevertheless true, that he did not advance very far in the general object. He was misled by the pursuit of a few surprising and paradoxical results, and when he had arrived at them he stopped.

After him, and at a short interval, appeared two philosophers, who were more sober-minded, and had better aims. These were Condillac and Hartley. The first work of Condillac appeared some years before the publication of that of Hartley; but the whole of Hartley's train of thought has so much the air of being his own, that there is abundant reason to believe the speculations of both philosophers equally original. They both began upon the ground that all simple ideas are copies of impressions; that all complex ideas are only simple ideas united by the principle of association. They proceeded to examine all the phenomena of the human mind, and were of opinion that the principle of association, or the succession of one simple idea after another, according to certain laws, accounts for the whole; that these laws might, by meditation, be ascertained and applied; and that then the human mind would be understood, as far as man has the means of knowing it.

The merit of Condillac is very great. It may yet, perhaps, be truer to say, that he wrote admirably upon philosophy, than that he was a great philosopher. His power consists in expression; he conveys metaphysical ideas with a union of brevity and clearness which never has been surpassed. But though he professed rather to deliver the opinions of others, than to aim at invention, it cannot be denied that he left the science of the human mind in a much better state than he found it; and this is equivalent to discovery. As a teacher, in giving, in this field, a right turn to the speculations of his countrymen, his value is incalculable; and there is, perhaps, no one human being, with the exception of Locke, who was his master, to whom, in this respect, the progress of the human mind is more largely indebted. It is also true, that to form the conception of tracing the sequences among our simple ideas, as comprehending the whole of the philosophy of the human mind, even with the helps which Hume had afforded, and it is more than probable that neither Condillac nor Hartley had ever heard of a work which, according to its author, had fallen dead-born from the press, was philosophical and sagacious in the highest degree.

It must be allowed, however, that, in expounding the various mental phenomena, Condillac does not display the same penetration and force of mind, or the same comprehensiveness, as Dr. Hartley. He made great *progress* in showing how those phenomena might be resolved into the sequences of simple ideas; but Dr. Hartley made still greater.

We do not mean to pronounce a positive opinion either for or against the grand undertaking of Dr. Hartley, to resolve the whole of the mental phenomena of man into sequences of impressions, and the simple ideas which are the copies of them. But we have no hesitation in saying, that he philosophizes with extraordinary power and sagacity; and it is astonishing how many of the mental phenomena he has clearly resolved; how little, in truth, he has left about which any doubt can remain.

We cannot afford to pursue this subject any farther. This much is ascertained,—that the character of the human mind consists in the sequences of its ideas; that the object of education, therefore, is, to provide for the constant production of certain sequences, rather than others; that we cannot be sure of adopting the best means to that end, unless we have the greatest knowledge of the sequences themselves.

In what has been already ascertained on this subject, we have seen that there are two things which have a wonderful power over those sequences. They are, Custom; and Pain and Pleasure. These are the grand instruments or powers, by the use of which, the purposes of education are to be attained.

Where one idea has followed another a certain number of times, the appearance of the first in the mind is sure to be followed by that of the second, and so on. One of the grand points, then, in the study of education, is to find the means of making, in the most perfect manner, those repetitions on which the beneficial sequences depend.

When we speak of making one idea follow another, and always that which makes part of a good train, instead of one that makes part of a bad train, there is one difficulty; that each idea, taken singly by itself, is as fit to be a part of a bad train as of a good one; for good trains and bad trains are both made out of the same simple elements. Trains, however, take place by sequences of twos, or threes, or any greater number; and the nature of these sequences, as complex parts of a still greater whole, is that which renders the train either salutary or hurtful. Custom is, therefore, to be directed to two points; first, to form those sequences, which make the component parts of a good train; and secondly, to join those sequences together, so as to constitute the trains.

When we speak of making one idea follow another, there must always be a starting point; there must be some one idea from which the train begins to flow; and it is pretty evident that much will depend upon this idea. One grand question, then, is, "What are the ideas which most frequently operate as the commencement of trains?" Knowing what are the ideas which play this important part, we may attach to them by custom, such trains as are the most beneficent. It has been observed that most, if not all, of our trains, start from a sensation, or some impression upon the external or internal nerves. The question then is, which are those sensations, or aggregates of sensations, which are of the most frequent recurrence? it being obviously of importance, that those which give occasion to the greatest number of trains, should be made, if possible, to give occasion only to the best trains. Now the sensations, or aggregates of sensations, which occur in the ordinary business of life, are those of most frequent recurrence; and from which it is of the greatest importance that beneficial trains should commence. Rising up in the morning, and going to bed at night, are aggregates of this description, common to all mankind; so are the commencement and termination of meals. The practical sagacity of priests, even in the rudest ages of the world, perceived the importance, for giving religious trains an ascendancy in the mind, of uniting them, by early and steady custom, with those perpetually recurring sensations. The morning and evening prayers, the grace before and after meals, have something correspondent to them in the religion of, perhaps, all nations.

It may appear, even from these few reflections and illustrations, that, if the sensations, which are most apt to give commencement to trains of ideas, are skilfully selected, and the trains which lead most surely to the happiness, first of the individual himself, and next of his fellow-creatures, are by custom effectually united with them, a provision of unspeakable importance is made for the happiness of the race.

Beside custom, it was remarked by Hobbs, that appetite had a great power over the mental trains. But appetite is the feeling toward pleasure or pain in prospect; that is, future pleasure or pain. To say that appetite, therefore, has power over the mental trains, is to say, that the prospect of pleasure or pain has. That this is true, every man knows by his own experience. The best means, then, of applying the prospect of pleasure and pain to render beneficent trains perpetual in the mind, is the discovery to be made, and to be recommended to mankind.

The way in which pleasure and pain affect the trains of the mind is, as ends. As a train commences in some present sensation, so it may be conceived as terminating in the idea of some future pleasure or pain. The intermediate ideas, between the commencement and the end, may be either of the beneficent description or the hurtful. Suppose the sight of a fine equipage to be the commencement, and the riches which afford it, the appetite, or the end of a train, in the mind of two individuals at the same time. The intermediate ideas in the mind of the one may be beneficent, in the other hurtful. The mind of the one immediately runs over all the honourable and useful modes of acquiring riches, the acquisition of the most rare and useful qualities, the eager watch of all the best opportunities of bringing them into action, and the steady industry with which they may be applied. That of the other recurs to none but the vicious modes of acquiring riches—by lucky accidents, the arts of the adventurer and impostor, by rapine and plunder, perhaps on the largest scale, by all the honours and glories of war. Suppose the one of these trains to be habitual among individuals, the other not: What a difference for mankind!

It is unnecessary to adduce farther instances for the elucidation of this part of our mental constitution. What, in this portion of the field, requires to be done for the science of education, appears to be, First, to ascertain, what are the ends, the really ultimate objects of human desire; Next, what are the most beneficent means of attaining those objects; and Lastly, to accustom the mind to fill up the intermediate space between the present sensation and the ultimate object, with nothing but the ideas of those beneficent means. We are perfectly aware that these instructions are far too general. But we hope it will be carried in mind, that little beyond the most general ideas can be embraced in so confined a sketch; and we are not without an expectation that, such as they are, these expositions will not be wholly without their use.

SECTION II

Qualities of Mind, to the Production of which the Business
of Education should be directed.

We come now to the second branch of the science of education, or the inquiry what are the qualities with which it is of most importance that the mind of the individual should be endowed. This enquiry we are in hopes the preceding exposition will enable us very materially to abridge.

In one sense, it might undoubtedly be affirmed, that all the desirable qualities of the human mind are included in those beneficent sequences of which we have spoken above. But, as it would require, to make this sufficiently intelligible, a more extensive exposition than we are able to afford, we must content ourselves with the ordinary language, and with a more familiar mode of considering the subject.

That intelligence is one of the qualities in question will not be denied, and may speedily be made to appear. To attain happiness is the object: and, to attain it in the greatest possible degree, all the means to that end, which the compass of nature affords, must be employed in the most perfect possible manner. But all the means which the compass of nature, or the system in which we are placed, affords, can only be known by the most perfect knowledge of that system. The highest measure of knowledge is therefore required. But mere knowledge is not enough; a mere magazine of remembered facts is an useless treasure. Amid the vast variety of known things, there is needed a power of choosing, a power of discerning which of them are conducive, which not, to the ends we have in view. The ingredients of intelligence are two, knowledge and sagacity; the one affording the materials upon which the other is to be exerted; the one, showing what exists; the other, converting it to the greatest use; the one, bringing within our ken what is capable, and what is not capable of being used as means; the other, seizing and combining, at the proper moment, whatever is fittest as means to each particular end. This union, then, of copiousness and energy; this possession of numerous ideas, with the masterly command of them, is one of the more immediate ends to which the business of education is to be directed.

With a view to happiness as the end, another quality will easily present itself as indispensable. Conceive that a man knows the materials which can be employed as means, and is prompt and unerring in the mode of combining them; all this power is lost, if there is any thing in his nature which prevents him from using it. If he has any appetite in his nature which leads him to pursue certain things with which the most effectual pursuit of happiness is inconsistent, so far this evil is incurred. A perfect command, then, over a man's appetites and desires; the power of restraining them whenever they lead in a hurtful direction; that possession of himself which insures his judgment against the illusions of the passions, and enables him to pursue constantly what he deliberately approves, is indispensably requisite to enable him to produce the greatest possible quantity of happiness. This is what the ancient philosophers called temperance; not exactly the same with what is called the virtue or grace of temperance, in theological morality, which includes a certain portion (in the doctrines of some theological instructors, a very large portion) of abstinence, and not only of abstinence, or the gratuitous renunciation of pleasure, but of the infliction of voluntary pain. This is done with a view to please the God, or object of worship, and to provide, through his favour, for the happiness of a second, or future life. The temperance of the ancient philosophers had a view only to the happiness of the present life, and consisted in the power of resisting the immediate propensity, if yielding to it would lead to an overbalance of evil or prevent the enjoyment of a superior good, in whatever the good or evil of the present life consists. This resisting power consists of two parts; the power of resisting pleasure, and that of resisting pain, the last of which has an appropriate name, and is called Fortitude.

These two qualities, the intelligence which can always choose the best possible means, and the strength which overcomes the misguiding propensities, appear to be sufficient for the happiness of the individual himself; to the pursuit of which it cannot be doubted that he always has sufficient motives. But education, we have said, should be an instrument to render the individual the best possible artificer of happiness, not to himself alone, but also to others. What, then, are the qualities with which he ought to be endowed, to make him produce the greatest possible quantity of happiness to others?

It is evident enough to see what is the first grand division. A man can affect the happiness of others, either by abstaining from doing them harm, or by doing them positive good. To abstain from doing them harm, receives the name of Justice; to do positive good receives that of Generosity. Justice and generosity, then, are the two qualities by which man is fitted to promote the happiness of his fellow-creatures. And it thus appears, that the four cardinal virtues of the ancients do pretty completely include all the qualities, to the possession of which it is desirable that the human mind should be trained. The defect, however, of this description is, that it is far too general. It is evident that the train of mental events which conduct to the proposed results must be far more particularized to insure, in any considerable degree, the effects of instruction; and it must be confessed that the ethical instructions of the ancients failed by remaining too much in generals. What is wanting is, that the incidents of human life should be skilfully classified; both those on the occasion of which they who are the objects of the good acts are pointed out for the receipt of them, and those on the occasion of which they who are to be the instruments are called upon for the performance. It thus appears that the science of Ethics, as well as the science of Intellectuals, must be carried to perfection, before the best foundation is obtained for the science of Education.

SECTION III

Happiness, the End to which Education is devoted.—Wherein it
consists, not yet determined.

We have spoken of the qualities which are subservient
to human happiness, as means to an end. But, before means
can be skilfully adapted to an end, the end must be accurately known. To know how the human mind is to be
trained to the promotion of happiness, another inquiry then,
is necessary; Wherein does human happiness consist? This
is a controverted question; and we have introduced it rather
with a view to show the place which it occupies in the
theory of education, than that we have it in our power to
elucidate a subject about which there is so much diversity
of opinion, and which some of the disputants lead into very
subtle and intricate inquiries. The importance of the question is sufficiently evident from this, that it is the grand
central point, to which all other questions and inquiries
converge; that point, by their bearing upon which, the
value of all other things is determined. That it should remain itself undetermined, implies, that this branch of philosophy is yet far from its highest point of perfection.

The speculations on this subject, too, may be divided
into two great classes; that of those who trace up all the
elements of happiness, as they do all those of intellect, to
the simple sensations which, by their transformation into
ideas, and afterwards into various combinations, compose,
they think, all the intellectual and moral phenomena of our
nature; another, that of those who are not satisfied with
this humble origin, who affirm that there is something in
human happiness, and in the human intellect, which soars
high above this corporeal level; that there are intellectual
as well as moral forms, the resplendent objects of human
desire, which can by no means be resolved into the grosser

elements of sense. These philosophers speak of eternal and immutable truths; truths which are altogether independent of our limited experience; which are truly universal; which the mind recognizes without the aid of the senses; and which are the objects of pure intellect. They affirm, also, that there is a notion of right and of wrong wholly underived from human experience, and independent of the laws which regulate, in this world, the happiness and misery of human life; a right and wrong, the distinction between which is perceived, according to some, by a peculiar sense; according to others, by the faculty which discerns pure truth; according to others, by common sense; it is the same, according to some, with the notion of the fitness and unfitness of things; according to others, with the law of nature; according to others, with truth; and there is one eminent philosopher who makes it depend upon sympathy, without determining very clearly whether sympathy depends upon the senses or not.

We cannot too earnestly exhort philosophers to perfect this inquiry; that we may understand at last, not by vague abstract terms, but clearly and precisely, what are the simple ideas included under the term happiness; and what is the real object to which education is pointed; since it is utterly impossible, while there is any vagueness and uncertainty with respect to the end, that there should be the greatest precision and certainty in combining the means.

SECTION IV

Instruments, and practical Expedients, of Education.

We come at last to the consideration of the means which are at the disposal of man for endowing the human mind with the qualities on which the generation of happiness depends. Under this head the discussion of the practical expedients chiefly occurs; but it also embraces some points of theory. The degree in which the useful qualities of human nature are, or are not, under the powers of education, is one of the most important.

This is the subject of a famous controversy, with names of the highest authority on both sides of the question. Helvetius, it is true, stands almost alone, on one side. But Helvetius, alone, is a host. No one man, perhaps, has done so much towards perfecting the *theory* of education as Mons. Helvetius; and his books are pregnant with information of the highest importance. Whoever wishes to understand the groundwork of education, can do nothing more conducive to his end, than to study profoundly the expositions of this philosophical inquirer, whether he adopts his conclusions, in all their latitude, or not. That Helvetius was not more admired in his own country, is owing really to the value of his work. It was too solid, for the frivolous taste of the gay circles of Paris, assemblies of pampered noblesse, who wished for nothing but amusement. That he has been so little valued, in this country, is, it must be confessed, owing a little to the same cause; but another has concurred. An opinion has prevailed, a false one, that Helvetius is a peculiarly dangerous enemy to religion; and this has deterred people from reading him; or rather the old people who do not read, have deterred the young who do. There is no book, the author of which does not disguise his unbelief, that can be read with more safety to religion. The author attacks nothing but priestcraft, and in one of the worst of its forms; the popish priestcraft of the dark and middle ages; the idea of which we are well accustomed, in this country, to separate from that of religion. When his phraseology at any time extends, and that is not often, to Christianity itself, or to religion in the abstract, there is nothing calculated to seduce. There is nothing epigrammatic, and sparkling in the expression; nothing sophistical and artfully veiled in the reasoning; a plain proposition is stated, with a plain indication of its evidence; and if your judgment is not convinced, you are not deluded through the fancy.

M. Helvetius says, that if you take men who bring into the world with them the original constituents of their nature, their mental and bodily frame, in that ordinary state of goodness which is common to the great body of mankind,—leaving out of the account the comparatively small number of individuals who come into the world imperfect, and manifestly below the ordinary standard,—you may regard the whole of this great mass of mankind, as equally susceptible of mental excellence; and may trace the causes which make them to differ. If this be so, the power of education embraces every thing between the lowest stage of intellectual and moral rudeness, and the highest state, not only of actual, but of possible perfection. And if the power of education be so immense, the motive for perfecting it is great beyond expression.

The conclusions of Helvetius were controverted directly by Rousseau; and defended, against the strictures of that writer, by the author himself. We recollect few writers in this country who have embraced them.* But our authors have contented themselves, rather with rejecting, than disproving; and, at best, have supported their rejection only by some incidental reflection, or the indication of a discrepancy between his conclusions and theirs.

One of the causes, why people have been so much startled, by the extent to which Helvetius has carried the dominion of education, seems to us to be their not including in it nearly so much as he does. They include in it little

---

* There is one brilliant authority on the side of Helvetius: "It was a favourite opinion of Sir Wm. Jones, that all men are born with an equal capacity of improvement."—Lord Teignmouth's *Life of Sir William Jones*, vol. ii, p. 211.

more than what is expressed by the term schooling; commencing about six or seven years of age, and ending at latest with the arrival of manhood. If this alone is meant by education, it is no doubt true, that education is far indeed from being all-powerful. But if in education is included every thing, which acts upon the being as it comes from the hand of nature, in such a manner as to modify the mind, to render the train of feelings different from what it would otherwise have been; the question is worthy of the most profound consideration. It is probable, that people in general form a very inadequate conception of all the circumstances which act during the first months, perhaps the first moments, of existence, and of the power of those circumstances in giving permanent qualities to the mind. The works of Helvetius would have been invaluable, if they had done nothing more than prove the vast importance of these circumstances, and direct towards them the attention of mankind. Rousseau began this important branch of the study of education. He remarked a variety of important facts, which, till his time, had been almost universally neglected, in the minds of infants, and how much might be done, by those who surround them, to give good or bad qualities to their minds, long before the time at which it had been supposed that education could commence. But Helvetius treated the subject much more profoundly and systematically. He traced the circumstances to the very moment of birth; he showed at how early an age indelible characters may be impressed; nay, that some of the circumstances over which man has a controul (for he speaks not of others), circumstances on which effects of the greatest importance depend, may be traced beyond the birth.

It is evident how much it imports the science of education, that these circumstances should, by careful and continued observation, be all ascertained, and placed in the order best adapted for drawing from them the most efficient practical rules. This is of more importance than determining the question, whether the prodigious difference, which exists among men ordinarily well organized, is owing wholly to the circumstances which have operated upon them since the first moment of their sensitive existence, or is in part produced by original peculiarities. Enough is ascertained to prove, beyond a doubt, that if education does not perform every thing, there is hardly anything which it does not perform: that nothing can be more fatal than the error of those who relax in the vigilance of education, because nature is powerful, and either renders it impossible for them to accomplish much, or accomplishes a great deal without them: that the feeling is much more conformable to experience, and much more conformable to utility, which ascribes every thing to education, and thus carries the motive for vigilance and industry, in that great concern, to its highest pitch. This much, at any rate, is ascertained, that all the difference which exists, or can ever be made to exist, between one *class* of men, and another, is wholly owing to education. Those peculiarities, if any such there be, which sink a man below, or elevate him above the ordinary state of aptitude to profit by education, have no operation in the case of large numbers, or bodies. But large numbers or bodies of men are raised to a high degree of mental excellence; and might, without doubt, be raised to still higher. Other large bodies, or whole nations, have been found in so very low a mental state, as to be little above the brutes. All this vast distance is undeniably the effect of education. This much, therefore, may be affirmed on the side of Helvetius, that a prodigious difference is produced by education; while, on the other hand, it is rather assumed than proved, that any difference exists, but that which difference of education creates.

Circumstances of the Physical Kind which operate upon the
Mind in the way of Education.

The circumstances which are included under the term
Education, in the comprehensive sense in which we have
defined it, may be divided, we have said, into Physical, and
Moral. We shall now consider the two classes in the order
in which we have named them; and have here again to
remind the reader, that we are limited to the task of pointing
out what we should wish to be done, rather than permitted
to attempt the performance.

Three things are desirable with regard to the physical
circumstances which operate in the way of education
favourably or unfavourably; to collect them fully; to appreciate them duly; and to place them in the order which is
most favourable for drawing from them practical rules.

This is a service (common to the sciences of education
and mind) which has been very imperfectly rendered. It
has been chiefly reserved to medical men to observe the
physical circumstances which affect the body and mind of
man; but of medical men few have been much skilled in
the observation of mental phenomena, or have thought
themselves called upon to mark the share which physical
circumstances had in producing them. There are indeed
some, and those remarkable, exceptions. There is Dr.
Darwin in our own country, and M. Cabanis in France.
They have both of them taken the mind as a part at least
of their study; and we are highly indebted to them for the
number and value of their observations. They are both
philosophers, in the most important sense of the word; they
both observed nature for themselves, observed her atten-
tively, and with their view steadily directed to the proper
end. But still it is not safe to rely upon them as guides.
They were in too great a haste to establish conclusions;
and were apt to let their belief run before their evidence.

They were not sufficiently careful to distinguish between the different degrees of evidence, and to mark what is required to constitute proof. To do this steadily seems, indeed, to be one of the rarest of all endowments; and was much less the characteristic of the two philosophers we have named, than a wise range of knowledge, from which they collected the facts, and great ingenuity in combining and applying them. Dr. Darwin was the most remarkable, both for the strength and the weakness of which we speak. The work of Darwin, to which we chiefly allude, is the *Zoönomia*; though important remarks to the same effect are scattered in his other publications. Cabanis entitled his great work, *Rapports du Physique et du Moral de l'Homme.* And there are some works recently announced by German physiologists, the titles of which promise aids in the same endeavour. But though we expect from them new facts, and ingenious hints, we have less hope of any great number of sound conclusions.

There are certain general names already in use, including the greater number of the physical circumstances which operate in the way of education upon the mind. It will be convenient, because of their commonness, to make use of them on the present occasion, though neither the enumeration which they make is complete, nor the distribution logical.

All the physical circumstances which operate upon the mind are either, 1. inherent in the body; or, 2. external to the body. Those which are external to the body, operate upon the mind, by first operating upon the body.

Of the first kind, the more remarkable seem to be healthiness or sickliness, strength or weakness, beauty or deformity, the temperament, the age, the sex.

Of the second sort, the more remarkable seem to be the aliment, the labour, the air, temperature, action, rest.

Previous to the inquiry concerning the power which physical circumstances exert in the formation of the mind, it may seem that we ought to determine the speculative question respecting the nature of the mind: that is, whether the phenomena of mind may possibly result from a certain organization of matter; or whether something of a different kind, and which we call spiritual, must not be conceived, as the source and organ of thought. We do not mean to enter into this controversy, which would detain us too long. It is not, in the least degree, necessary, for the end which we have in view. Whether the one hypothesis, with respect to the mind, be adopted, or the other, the distribution of the circumstances, which operate in the formation of human character, into those commonly called Physical, and those commonly called Moral, will be as convenient as any distribution which the present state of our knowledge enables us to make; and all that inquiry can do, in regard to those circumstances, is, to trace them accurately, and to observe their effects; that is, to ascertain what they are, and what the order of the mental events by which they are followed. This is simply matter of experience; and what we experience is the same, whether we adopt one opinion, or another, with regard to the nature of that which thinks. It is in what we experience, all ascertained, and put into the best possible shape for ease of comprehension, and ready application to practice, that all useful knowledge on this, as on all other subjects, consists.

1. First, we are to consider the circumstances of the body which have an effect upon the mental sequences. The object is, to ascertain which have a tendency to introduce those sequences which are favourable, which to introduce those that are unfavourable, to human happiness, and how to turn this knowledge to account.

Health and sickness, or the states of body which those

names most peculiarly express, are the first of the circumstances which we have enumerated under this head. That these states have a tendency to introduce very different trains of thought, is matter of vulgar experience; but very little has been done to examine such trains, and to ascertain what in each is favourable, and what is unfavourable to human happiness.

We have already seen, that the trains which are favourable to Intelligence, Temperance, Justice, and Generosity, are the trains favourable to human happiness. Now, with respect to Intelligence, it will be seen, that Health is partly favourable, and partly unfavourable; and the same is the case with Sickness. Health is favourable, by allowing that time to be given to study, which many kinds of sickness withdraw, and by admitting a more vigorous attention, which the pain and languor of sickness often impair. It is unfavourable, by introducing that flow of pleasurable ideas which is called high spirits, adverse at a certain pitch to the application of attention; and by leading to that passionate pursuit of pleasure, which diminishes, if it does not destroy, the time for study. The mode in which disease operates upon the mental sequences is a subject of great complexity, and in which little has yet been done to mark distinctly the events, and ascertain the order of their succession. Cabanis, in his seventh memoir, entitled, *De l'Influence des Maladies sur la Formation des Idées et des Affections Morales*, has made a useful beginning toward the elucidation of this subject; but here, as elsewhere, he is too often general and vague. Instruction may also be gleaned from Darwin; but the facts which bear upon this point rather drop from him incidentally, than are anywhere put together systematically for its elucidation. As they were both physicians, however, of great experience, and of unusual skill in the observation of mental phenomena, their opinions are entitled to the greatest respect. The result of the matter is, that an improved medicine is no trifling branch of the art and science of education. Cabanis, accordingly, concludes his memoir with the two following propositions:

"1mo. L'état de maladie influe d'une manière directe sur la formation des idées et des affections morales: nous avons même pu montrer dans quelques observations particulières, comment cette influence s'exerce.

"2do. L'observation et l'expérience nous ayant fait découvrir les moyens de combattre assez souvent avec succès l'état de maladie, l'art qui met en usage ces moyens, peut donc modifier et perfectionner les opérations de l'intelligence et les habitudes de la volonté."

As it is chiefly through the nervous system, and the centre of that system, the brain, that the mental sequences are affected, and as all the sensitive parts have not an action equally strong, nor equally direct, upon the nerves and brain, diseases affect the mental sequences differently, according to the parts which they invade. The system of the nerves and brain is itself subject to different states of disease. Classified with regard to the functions which that system performs, as the organ of sensibility and of action, these states are thus described by M. Cabanis: "1. Excess of sensibility to all impressions on the one part; excessive action on the organs of motion on the other. 2. Unfitness to receive impressions, in sufficient number, or with the due degree of energy; and a diminution of the activity necessary for the production of the motions. 3. A general disturbance of the functions of the system, without any remarkable appearance of either excess or defect. 4. A bad distribution of the cerebral virtue, either when it exerts itself unequally in regard to time, having fits of extraordinary activity, followed by others of considerable remission; or when it is supplied in wrong proportion to the different organs, of which some are to a great degree abandoned, while there appears in others a concentration of sensibility, and of the excitations or powers by which the movements are affected."

The effects upon the mental sequences are represented in the following general sketch, which has the advantage of being tolerably comprehensive, though it is unhappily both vague and confused: "We may lay it down as a general fact, that, in all the marked affections of the nerves, irregularities, less or greater, take place, relative both to the mode in which impressions are received, and to the mode in which the determinations, automatic or voluntary, are formed. On one part, the sensations vary incessantly and rapidly with respect to their vivacity, their energy, and even their number; on another, the strength, the readiness, the facility of action exhibit the greatest inequalities. Hence perpetual fluctuation, from great excitement to languor, from elevation to dejection; a temper and passions variable in the highest degree. In this condition, the mind is always easily pushed to extremes. Either the man has many ideas, with great mental activity and acuteness; or, he is, on the contrary, almost incapable of thinking. It has been well observed, that hypochondriacal persons are by turns both courageous and cowardly; and as the impressions are habitually faulty either by excess or defect, in regard to almost all objects, it is seldom that the images correspond to the reality of things; that the desires and the will obtain the proper force and direction. If, along with these irregularities, which arise from the nervous system, should be found a weakness of the muscular organs, or of some important viscus, as, for example, of the stomach,—the phenomena, though still analogous in the main, will be distinguished by remarkable peculiarities. During the interval of languor, the debility of the muscles renders the sense of weakness, the fainting and drooping, still more complete and oppressive; life appears ready to escape at every instant. The passions are gloomy, excited by trifles, selfish; the ideas are petty, narrow, and bear only upon the objects of the slightest sensations. At the times of excitation, which arrive the more suddenly the greater the weakness; the muscular determinations do not obey the impulses of the brain, unless by starts, which have neither energy nor duration. These impulses serve only to convince the patient more profoundly of his real imbecility; they give him only a feeling of impatience, of discontent, and anxiety. Desires, often sufficiently keen, but commonly repressed by the habitual feeling of weakness, still more increase the discouraging impression. As the peculiar organ of thought cannot act without the concurrence of several others, and as, at that moment, it partakes in some degree of the weakness which affects the organs of movement, the ideas present themselves in crowds; they spring up, but do not arrange themselves in order; the necessary attention is not enjoyed; the consequence is, that this activity of the imagination, which we might expect to afford some compensation for the absence of other faculties, becomes a new source of dejection and despair."

In this passage, the mental sequences which particular states of disease introduce are clearly shown to have a prodigious influence upon human happiness; but the effects which are produced in respect to intelligence, temperance, generosity and justice, are mixed up together; and the author rather shows how much this subject deserves to be studied, than gives us information from which any considerable degree of practical utility can be derived. The connection between particular states of body, and particular mental trains, ought to be carefully watched and recorded. When the events, one by one, are accurately distinguished, and made easy to be recognized, and when the order in which they follow one another is known, our power over the trains of those events, power to prevent such as are unfavourable, to produce such as are favourable, to human happiness, will then be at its height; and how to take care of his health will be one of the leading parts of the moral and intellectual education of man.

The state of the body, with regard to health and disease, is the inherent circumstance of the greatest importance, and we must pass over the rest with a cursory notice. The next we mentioned, are, Strength and Weakness, meaning chiefly muscular strength and weakness; and the natural, habitual, not the accidental, or diseased, state. It is a common observation, that muscular strength is apt to withdraw the owner from mental pursuits, and engage him in such as are more of the animal kind; the acquisition and display of physical powers. Few men of great bodily powers have been much distinguished for mental excellence; some of the greatest ornaments of human nature have been remarkable for bodily weakness. Muscular strength is liable to operate unfavourably upon the moral as well as the intellectual trains of thought. It diminishes that respect for other men, which is so necessary to resist the impulses of passion; it presents innumerable occasions for playing the tyrant with impunity; and fosters, therefore, all that train of ideas, in which the tyrannical vices are engendered. Cabanis remarks, and the fact is worthy of the greatest attention,—"Presque tous les grands scélérats sont des hommes d'une structure organique vigoureuse, remarquables par la fermeté et la ténacité de leurs fibres musculaires." It is evident, therefore, how deeply it concerns the happiness of mankind, that the mental trains, which this circumstance has a tendency to raise, should be accurately known, as thus alone the means can be known, how that which is hurtful may be avoided, that which is useful be introduced.

Of beauty and deformity, as circumstances affecting the mental trains, much will not be necessary to be said. Illustrations will occur to every body, to prove, that their power is not inconsiderable; so little, however, has been done to ascertain the facts, and record them in the best possible order, that any thing which deserves the name of knowledge on the subject hardly exists; and the principal service we can render is to point it out for study; to exhort future inquirers to observe diligently the trains which flow from beauty and deformity as their source, and to trace to the largest possible sequences, as above described, the connections which take place between them. Beauty and deformity, it may be observed, operate upon the mental trains in somewhat a different way from health and disease; rather mediately than immediately. It is the idea of their effect upon other people that is the more immediate cause of the trains to which they give occasion. The idea that beauty commands their favourable regards, is apt to introduce the well known trains, denoted by the terms, vanity, pride, contemptuousness, trains not very favourable to the virtues. The idea that deformity is apt to excite their unfavourable regards, is often observed to lead to acuteness and vigour of intellect, employed as instruments of protection, but to moroseness, and even malignity of temper. The mode, however, in which beauty and deformity operate upon the mental trains, namely, through the idea of their effect upon other people, is common to them with a great many other advantages or disadvantages, which derive their value chiefly from their influence upon other people; and materials for the illustration of this subject have been supplied by various writers upon the human mind.

To the word Temperament, no very precise idea has

hitherto been annexed. It may be conceived in the following manner: The bodily structure, the composition of elements in the body of every individual, is different from that in the body of any other. It is observed, however, that the composition is more nearly resembling in some, than in others; that those who thus resemble may be arranged in groups; and that they may all be comprehended in four or five great classes. The circumstances, in which their bodily composition agrees, so as to constitute one of those large classes, have been called the Temperament; and each of those more remarkable characters of the body has been observed to be attended with a peculiar character in the train of ideas. But the illustration of the trains of ideas, and hence of the qualities of mind, which are apt to be introduced by temperament, and by the diversities of age and of sex, we are obliged, by the rapid absorption of the space allotted us, wholly to omit. The subject in itself is not very mysterious. Accurate observation, and masterly recordation alone are required. To be sure, the same may be said of every object of human inquiry. But in some cases, it is not so easy to conceive perfectly what observation and recordation mean. On these topics, also, we are happy to say, that Cabanis really affords very considerable helps.

2. We come now to the second sort of physical circumstances, which have the power of introducing habitually certain trains of ideas, and hence of impressing permanent tendencies on the mind,—the circumstances which are external to the body.- Some of these are of very great importance. The first is Aliment.

Aliment is good or evil, by quality and quantity. Hartley has remarked long ago, that though all the impressions from which ideas are copied, are made on the extremities of the nerves which are ramified on the surface of the body,

and supply the several organs of sense, other impressions
are nevertheless made on the extremities of the nerves which
are ramified on the internal parts of our bodies, and that
many of those impressions are associated with trains of
ideas; that the impressions made upon the extremities of
the nerves which are ramified on the alimentary canal, are
associated with the greatest number of those trains; and of
such trains, that some are favourable to happiness, some
altogether the reverse. If the quantity and quality of the
aliment be the principal cause of those impressions, here
is a physiological reason, of the greatest importance, for an
accurate observation and recordation of the events occurring
in this part of the field; what antecedents are attended by
what consequents, and what the largest sequences that can
be traced. Cabanis confirmed the doctrine of Hartley with
regard to the internal impressions, and added another class.
He said that not only the extremities of the nerves which
terminate internally, but the centre of the nervous influence,
the brain itself, received impressions, and that thus there
were no fewer than three sources of mental and corporeal
movements of man; one external, from which almost all
our distinct ideas are copied; and two internal, which
exert a very great influence upon the trains of ideas, and
hence upon the actions of which these trains are the antecedents or cause.

On this too, as on most of the other topics, belonging
to the physical branch of education, we must note, as still
uncollected, the knowledge which is required. It is understood in a general way, that deep impressions are by this
means made upon the mind; but how they are made, is a
knowledge which, in any such detail and accuracy as to
afford useful practical rules, is nearly wanting. There is a
passage in Hartley, which we esteem it important to quote:
"The sense of feeling may be distinguished into that of the

external surface of the body, and that of the cavities of the nose, mouth, fauces, alimentary duct, pelvis, of the kidneys, uterus, bladder of urine, gall bladder, follicles, and ducts of the glands, &c. The sensibility is much greater in the last than in the first, because the impressions can more easily penetrate through the soft epithelium with which the internal cavities are invested. In the mouth and nose this sensibility is so great, and attended with such distinguishing circumstances, as to have the names of taste and smell assigned respectively to the sensations impressed upon the papillæ of these two organs.... The taste may also be distinguished into two kinds; viz. the general one which extends itself to the insides of the lips and cheeks, to the palate, fauces, æsophagus, stomach, and whole alimentary duct, quite down to the anus.... The pleasures of the taste, considered as extending itself from the mouth through the whole alimentary duct, are very considerable, and frequently repeated; they must, therefore, be one chief means by which pleasurable states are introduced into the brain and nervous system. These pleasurable states must, after some time, leave miniatures of themselves, sufficiently strong to be called up upon slight occasions, viz. from a variety of associations with the common visible and audible objects, and to illuminate these and their ideas. When groups of these miniatures have been long and closely connected with particular objects, they coalesce into one complex idea, appearing, however, to be a simple one; and so begin to be transferred upon other objects, and even upon tastes back again, and so on without limits. And from this way of reasoning it may now appear, that a great part of our intellectual pleasures are ultimately deducible from those of taste; and that one principal final cause of the greatness and constant recurrency of these pleasures, from our first infancy to the extremity of old age, is to introduce and keep up pleasurable states in the brain, and to connect them with foreign objects. The social pleasures seem, in a particular manner, to be derived from this source, since it has been customary in all ages and nations, and is in a manner necessary, that we should enjoy the pleasures of taste in conjunction with our relations, friends, and neighbours. In like manner, nauseous tastes and painful impressions upon the alimentary duct give rise and strength to mental pains. The most common of these painful impressions is that from excess, and the consequent indigestion. This excites and supports those uneasy states, which attend upon melancholy, fear, and sorrow. It appears also to me, that these states are introduced in a great degree during sleep, during the frightful dreams, agitations, and oppressions, that excess in diet occasions in the night. These dreams and disorders are often forgotten; but the uneasy states of body which then happen, leave vestiges of themselves, which increase in number and strength every day from the continuance of the cause, till at last they are ready to be called up in crowds upon slight occasions, and the unhappy person is unexpectedly, and at once, as it were, seized with a great degree of the hypochondriac distemper, the obvious cause appearing no ways proportionable to the effect. And thus it may appear that there ought to be a great reciprocal influence between the mind and alimentary duct, agreeably to common observation." Cabanis, in like manner, says, "Quoique les médecins aient dit plusieurs choses hazardées, touchant l'effet des substances alimentaires sur les organes de la pensée, ou sur les principes physiques de nos penchans, il n'en est pas moins certain que les différentes causes que nous appliquons journellement à nos corps, pour en renouveler les mouvements, agissent avec une grande efficacité sur nos dispositions morales. On se rend plus propre aux travaux de l'esprit par certaines précautions de régime, par l'usage, ou la suppression de certains alimens. Quelques personnes ont été guéries de violens accès de colère, auxquels elles étoient sujettes, par la seule diète pythagorique, et dans le cas même ou des délires furieux troublent toutes les facultés de l'âme, l'emploi journalier de certaines nourritures ou de certaines boissons, l'impression d'une certaine température de l'air, l'aspect de certaines objets; en un mot, un système diététique particulier suffit souvent pour y ramener le calme, pour faire tout rentrer dans l'ordre primitif."

As it is impossible for us here to attempt a full account of the mode in which aliments operate to produce good or bad effects upon the train of ideas, we shall single out that case, which, as operating upon the greatest number of people, is of the greatest importance; we mean that, in which effects are produced by the *poverty* of the diet; proposing, under the term poverty, to include both badness of quality, and defect of quantity. On badness of quality, we shall not spend many words. Aliments are bad in a variety of ways, and to such a degree as to impair the bodily health. Of such, the injurious effect will not be disputed. Others, which have in them no hurtful ingredient, may contain so insignificant a portion of nourishment, that to afford it in the requisite degree, they must produce a hurtful distention of the organs. The saw-dust, which some northern nations use for bread, if depended upon for the whole of their nourishment, would doubtless have this effect. The potatoe, where solely depended upon, is not, perhaps, altogether free from it. Bad quality, however, is but seldom resorted to, except in consequence of deficient quantity. That is, therefore, the principal point of inquiry.

It is easy to see a great number of ways in which deficient quantity of food operates unfavourably upon the *moral* temper of the mind. As people are ready to sacrifice every

thing to the obtaining of a sufficient quantity of food, the
want of it implies the most dreadful poverty; that state, in
which there is scarcely any source of pleasure, and in which
almost every moment is subject to pain. It is found by a
very general experience, that a human being, almost constantly in pain, hardly visited by a single pleasure, and
almost shut out from hope, loses by degrees all sympathy
with his fellow creatures; contracts even a jealousy of their
pleasures, and at last a hatred; and would like to see all the
rest of mankind as wretched as himself. If he is habitually
wretched, and rarely permitted to taste a pleasure, he
snatches it with an avidity, and indulges himself with an
intemperance, almost unknown to any other man. The evil
of insufficient food acts with an influence not less malig-
nant upon the intellectual, than upon the moral part of the
human mind. The physiologists account for its influence
in this manner. They say, that the signs, by which the living
energy is manifested, may be included generally under the
term *irritability*, or the power of being put in action by
stimulants. It is not necessary for us to be very particular
in explaining these terms; a general conception will for the
present suffice. A certain degree of this irritability seems
necessary to the proper state, or rather the very existence
of the animal functions. A succession of stimulants, of a
certain degree of frequency and strength, is necessary to
preserve that irritability. The most important by far of all
the useful stimulants applied to the living organs is food.
If this stimulant is applied, in less than a sufficient degree,
the irritability is diminished in proportion, and all those
manifestations of the living energy which depend upon it,
mental as well as corporeal, are impaired; the mind loses
a corresponding part of its force. We must refer to the
philosophical writers on medicine for illustrations and facts,
which we have not room to adduce, but which will not be

difficult to collect. Dr. Crichton places *poor diet* at the head of a list of causes which "weaken attention, and consequently debilitate the whole faculties of the mind."* From this fact, about which there is no dispute, the most important consequences arise. It follows, that when we deliberate about the means of introducing intellectual and moral excellence, into the minds of the principal portion of the people, one of the first things which we are bound to provide for, is, a generous and animating diet. The physical causes must go along with the moral; and nature herself forbids, that you shall make a wise and virtuous people, out of a starving one. Men must be happy themselves, before they can rejoice in the happiness of others; they must have a certain vigour of mind, before they can, in the midst of habitual suffering, resist a presented pleasure; their own lives, and means of well-being, must be worth something, before they can value, so as to respect, the life, or well-being, of any other person. This or that individual may be an extraordinary individual, and exhibit mental excellence in the midst of wretchedness; but a wretched and excellent people never yet has been seen on the face of the earth. Though far from fond of paradoxical expressions, we are tempted to say, that a good diet is a necessary part of a good education; for in one very important sense it is emphatically true. In the great body of the people all education is impotent without it.

Labour is the next of the circumstances in our enumeration. We have distinguished labour from action, though action is the genus of which labour is one of the species; because of those species, labour is so much the most important. The muscular operations of the body, by which men generally earn their bread, are the chief part of the

* *An Inquiry into the Nature and Origin of Mental Derangement.* &c. By A. Crichton, M.D. 1. 274.

particulars which we include under that term. The same distinction is useful here as in the former case; labour is apt to be injurious by its *quality*, and by its *quantity*. That the quality of the labour, in which a man is employed, produces effects, favourable or unfavourable upon his mind, has long been confessed; Dr. Smith made the important remark, that the labour in which the great body of the people are employed, has a tendency to grow less and less favourable, as civilization and the arts proceed. The division and sub-division of labour is the principal cause. This confines the attention of the labourer to so small a number of objects, and so narrow a circle of ideas, that the mind receives not that varied exercise, and that portion of aliment, on which almost every degree of mental excellence depends. When the greater part of a man's life is employed in the performance of a few simple operations, in one fixed invariable course, all exercise of ingenuity, all adaptation of means to ends, is wholly excluded, and the faculty lost, as far as disuse can destroy the faculties of the mind. The minds, therefore, of the great body of the people are in danger of really degenerating, while the other elements of civilization are advancing, unless care is taken, by means of the other instruments of education, to counteract those effects which the simplification of the manual processes has a tendency to produce.

The *quantity* of labour is another circumstance which deserves attention in estimating the agents which concur in forming the mind. Labour may be to such a degree severe, as to confine the attention almost wholly to the painful ideas which it brings; and to operate upon the mind with nearly the same effects as an habitual deficiency of food. It operates perhaps still more rapidly; obliterating sympathy, inspiring cruelty and intemperance, rendering impossible the reception of ideas, and paralyzing the organs of the mind. The attentive examination, therefore, of the facts of this case, is a matter of first-rate importance. Two things are absolutely certain; that without the bodily labour of the great bulk of mankind the well-being of the species cannot be obtained; and that if the bodily labour of the great bulk of mankind is carried beyond a certain extent, neither intellect, virtue, nor happiness can flourish upon the earth. What, then, is that precious middle point, at which the greatest quantity of good is obtained with the smallest quantity of evil, is, in this part of the subject, the problem to be solved.

The state of defective food and excessive labour, is the state in which we find the great bulk of mankind; the state in which they are either constantly existing, or into which they are every moment threatening to fall. These are two, therefore, in settling the rank among the circumstances which concur in determining the degree of intellect and morality capable of being exhibited in the societies of men, which ought to stand in a very eminent place: the mode of increasing to the utmost, the quantity of intellect, morality, and happiness, in human society, will be very imperfectly understood, till they obtain a new degree of consideration.

We named, besides these, among the physical circumstances which contribute to give permanent characters to the mind, air, temperature, action, and rest. But of these we must leave the illustration wholly to other inquirers. It is mortifying to be obliged to relinquish a subject, on which so much depends, and for which so little has been done, with so very imperfect an attempt for its improvement. We shall, however, have performed a service of some utility to education, if what we have said has any tendency to lead men to a juster estimate of the physical circumstances which concur in fashioning the human mind, and hence to greater industry and care in studying and applying them.

The Moral circumstances which determine the mental trains of the human being, and hence the character of his actions, are of so much importance, that to them the term education has been generally confined: or rather, the term education has been generally used in so narrow a sense, that it embraces only one of the four classes into which we have thought it convenient to distribute the moral circumstances which operate to the formation of the human mind.

1. The first of these classes we have comprehended under the term DOMESTIC EDUCATION. To this the groundwork of the character of most individuals is almost wholly to be traced. The original features are fabricated here; not, indeed, in such a manner as to be unsusceptible of alteration, but in such a manner, decidedly, as to present a good or bad subject for all future means of cultivation. The importance, therefore, of domestic education, needs no additional words to explain it; though it is difficult to restrain a sigh, when we reflect, that it has but now begun to be regarded as within the pale of education; and a few scattered remarks, rather than a full exposition of the subject, is all the information upon it, with which the world has been favoured.

By Domestic Education, we denote all that the child hears and sees, more especially all that it is made to suffer or enjoy at the hands of others, and all that it is allowed or constrained to do, in the house in which it is born and bred, which we shall consider, generally, as the parental.

If we consider, that the mental trains, as explained above, are that upon which every thing depends, and that the mental trains depend essentially upon those sequences among our sensations which have been so frequently experienced as to create a habit of passing from the idea of the one to that of the other, we shall perceive immediately the reasons of what we have advanced.

It seems to be a law of human nature, that the first sensations experienced produce the greatest effects; more especially, that the earliest repetitions of one sensation after another produce the deepest habit; the strongest propensity to pass immediately from the idea of the one to the idea of the other. Common language confirms this law, when it speaks of the susceptibility of the tender mind. On this depends the power of those associations which form some of the most interesting phenomena of human life. From what other cause does it arise, that the hearing of a musical air, which, after a life of absence, recalls the parental mansion, produces as it were a revolution in the whole being? That the sympathies between brothers and sisters are what they are? On what other cause originally is the love of country founded?—that passionate attachment to the soil, the people, the manners, the woods, the rivers, the hills, with which our infant eyes were familiar, which fed our youthful imaginations, and with the presence of which the pleasures of our early years were habitually conjoined!

It is, then, a fact, that the early sequences to which we are accustomed form the primary habits; and that the primary habits are the fundamental character of the man. The consequence is most important; for it follows, that, as soon as the infant, or rather the embryo, begins to feel, the character begins to be formed; and that the habits, which are then contracted, are the most pervading and operative of all. Education, then, or the care of forming the habits, ought to commence, as much as possible, with the period of sensation itself; and, at no period, is its utmost vigilance of greater importance, than the first.

Very unconnected, or very general instructions, are all that can be given upon this subject, till the proper decompositions and recompositions are performed; in other words, till the subject is first analyzed, and then systemized; or, in one word, *philosophized*, if we may use that verb in a passive signification. We can, therefore, do little more than exhort to the prosecution of the inquiry.

The steady conception of the End must guide us to the Means. Happiness is the end; and we have circumscribed the inquiry, by naming Intelligence, Temperance, and Benevolence, of which last the two parts are Generosity and Justice, as the grand qualities of mind, through which this end is to be attained. The question, then, is, how can those early sequences be made to take place on which the habits, conducive to intelligence, temperance, and benevolence, are founded; and how can those sequences, on which are founded the vices opposite to those virtues, be prevented?

Clearness is attained, by disentangling complexity; we ought, therefore, to trace the sequences conducive to each of those qualities in their turn. A part, however, must suffice when we cannot accomplish the whole. Intelligent trains of ideas constitute intelligence. Trains of ideas are intelligent, when the sequences in the ideas correspond to the sequences in nature. A man, for example, knows the order of certain words, when his idea of the one follows that of the other, in the same order in which the events themselves took place. A man is sagacious in devising means for the production of events when his ideas run easily in trains which are at once agreeable to knowledge, that is, to the trains of events, and at the same time new in the combination. They must be agreeable to knowledge; that is, one of the ideas must follow another in the order in which the objects of which they are the ideas follow one another in nature, otherwise the train would consist of mere chimeras, and, having no connection with things, would be utterly useless. As the event, however, is not in the ordinary course; otherwise sagacity would not be required to give it existence; the ordinary train of antecedents will not suffice; it must be a peculiar train, at once correspondent with nature, and adapted to the end. The earliest trains, produced in the minds of children, should be made to partake as much as possible of those characters. The impressions made upon them should correspond to the great and commanding sequences established among the events on which human happiness principally depends. More explicitly, children ought to be made to see, and hear, and feel, and taste, in the order of the most invariable and comprehensive sequences, in order that the ideas which correspond to their impressions, and follow the same order of succession, may be an exact transcript of nature, and always lead to just anticipations of events. Especially, the pains and pleasures of the infant, the deepest impressions which he receives, ought, from the first moment of sensation, to be made as much as possible to correspond to the real order of nature. The moral procedure of parents is directly the reverse; they strive to defeat the order of nature in accumulating pleasures for their children, and preventing the arrival of pains, when the children's own conduct would have had very different effects.

Not only are the impressions, from which ideas are copied, made, by the injudicious conduct of those to whom the destiny of infants is confided, to follow an order very different from the natural one, or that in which the grand sequences among events would naturally produce them; but wrong trains of ideas, trains which have no correspondence with the order of events, are often introduced immediately by words, or other signs of the ideas of other men. As we can only give very partial examples of a general error, we may content ourselves with one of the most common. When those who are about children express by their words, or indicate by other signs, that terrific trains of ideas are passing in their minds, when they go into the dark; terrific trains, which have nothing to do with the order of events, come up also in the minds of the children in the dark, and often exercise over them an uncontrollable sway during the whole of their lives.——This is the grand source of wrong education; to this may be traced the greater proportion of all the evil biases of the human mind.——If an order of ideas, corresponding with the order of events, were taught to come up in the minds of children when they go into the dark, they would think of nothing but the real dangers which are apt to attend it, and the precautions which are proper to be taken; they would have no wrong feelings, and their conduct would be nothing but that which prudence, or a right conception of the events, would prescribe. ——If the expressions, and other signs of the ideas of those who are about children, indicate that trains, accompanied with desire and admiration, pass in their minds when the rich and powerful are named, trains accompanied with aversion and contempt when the weak and the poor, the foundation is laid of a character stained with servility to those above, and tyranny to those below them. If indication is given to children that ideas of disgust, of hatred, and detestation, are passing in the minds of those about them, when particular descriptions of men are thought of; as men of different religions, different countries, or different political parties in the same country; a similar train becomes habitual in the minds of the children; and those antipathies are generated which infuse so much of its bitterness into the cup of human life.

We can afford to say but very few words on the powers of domestic education with regard to Temperance. That virtue bears a reference to pain and pleasure. The grand object evidently is, to connect with each pain and pleasure those trains of ideas which, according to the order established among events, tend most effectually to increase the sum of pleasures upon the whole, and diminish that of pains. If the early trains create a habit of over-valuing any pleasure or pain, too much will be sacrificed, during life, to obtain the one, or avoid the other, and the sum of happiness, upon the whole, will be impaired. The order in which children receive their impressions, as well as the order of the trains which they copy from others, has a tendency to create impatience under privation; in other words, to make them in prodigious haste to realize a pleasure as soon as desired, to extinguish a pain as soon as felt. A pleasure, however, can be realized in the best possible manner, or a pain removed, only by certain steps,—frequently numerous ones; and if impatience hurries a man to overlook those steps, he may sacrifice more than he gains. The desirable thing would be, that his ideas should always run over those very steps, and none but them; and the skilful use of the powers we have over the impressions and trains of his infancy would lay the strongest foundation for the future happiness of himself, and of all those over whom his actions have any sway. It is by the use of this power that almost every thing is done to create what is called the temper of the individual; to render him irascible on the one hand, or forbearing on the other; severe and unforgiving, or indulgent and placable.

Intelligence and Temperance are sometimes spoken of, as virtues which have a reference to the happiness of the individual himself: Benevolence as a virtue which has a reference to the happiness of others. The truth is, that intelligence and temperance have a reference not less direct to the happiness of others than to that of the possessor; and Benevolence cannot be considered as less essential to his happiness than intelligence and temperance. In reality, as the happiness of the individual is bound up with that of his species, that which affects the happiness of the one, must also, in general, affect that of the other.

It is not difficult, from the expositions we have already given, to conceive in a general way how sequences may take place in the mind of the infant which are favourable to benevolence, and how sequences may take place which are unfavourable to it. The difficulty is, so to bring forward and exhibit the details, as to afford the best possible instruction for practice. We have several books now in our own language, in particular those of Miss Edgeworth, which afford many finely selected instances, and many detached observations of the greatest value, for the cultivation of benevolence in the infant mind. But the great task of the philosopher, that of *theorizing* the whole, is yet to be performed. What we mean by "theorizing the whole," after the explanations we have already afforded, is not, we should hope, obscure. It is, to observe exactly the facts; to make a perfect collection of them, nothing omitted that is of any importance, nothing included of none; and to record them in that order and form, in which all that is best to be done in practice can be most immediately and certainly perceived.

The order of the impressions which are made upon the child, by the spontaneous order of events, is, to a certain degree, favourable to benevolence. The pleasures of those who are about him are most commonly the cause of pleasure to himself; their pains of pain. When highly pleased, they are commonly more disposed to exert themselves to gratify him. A period of pain or grief in those about him, is a period of gloom—a period in which little is done for pleasure—a period in which the pleasures of the child are apt to be overlooked. Trains of pleasurable ideas are thus apt to arise in his mind, at the thought of the pleasurable condition of those around him; trains of painful ideas at the thought of the reverse; and he is thus led to have an habitual desire for the one, aversion to the other. But if pleasures, whencesoever derived, of those about him, are apt to be the cause of good to himself, those pleasures which they derive from himself, are in a greater degree the cause of good to himself. If those about him are disposed to exert themselves to please him when they are pleased themselves, they are disposed to exert themselves in a much greater degree to please him, in particular, when it is he who is the cause of the pleasure they enjoy. A train of ideas, in the highest degree pleasurable, may thus habitually pass through his mind at the thought of happiness to others produced by himself; a train of ideas, in the highest degree painful, at the thought of misery to others produced by himself. In this manner the foundation of a life of beneficence is laid.

The business of a skilful education is, so to arrange the circumstances by which the child is surrounded, that the impressions made upon him shall be in the order most conducive to this happy result. The impressions, too, which are made originally upon the child, are but one of the causes of the trains which are rendered habitual to him, and which, therefore, obtain a leading influence in his mind. When he is often made to conceive the trains of other men, by the words, or other signs by which their feelings are betokened, those borrowed trains become also habitual, and exert a similar influence on the mind. This, then, is another of the instruments of education. When the trains, signified to the child, of the ideas in the minds of those about him are trains of pleasure at the thought of the happiness of other human beings, trains of the opposite kind at the conception of their misery; and when such trains are still more pleasurable or

painful as the happiness or misery is produced by themselves,
the association becomes in time sufficiently powerful to
govern the life.

The grand object of human desire is a command over
the wills of other men. This may be attained, either by
qualities and acts which excite their love and admiration,
or by those which excite their terror. When the education
is so wisely conducted as to make the train run habitually
from the conception of the good end to the conception of
the good means; and as often, too, as the good means are
conceived, viz. the useful and beneficial qualities, to make
the train run on to the conception of the great reward, the
command over the wills of men; an association is formed
which impels the man through life to pursue the great object
of desire, by fitting himself to be, and by actually becoming,
the instrument of the greatest possible benefit to his fellow
men.

But, unhappily, a command over the wills of men may
be obtained by other means than by doing them good; and
these, when a man can command them, are the shortest,
the easiest and the most effectual. These other means are
all summed up in a command over the pains of other men.
When a command over the wills of other men is pursued
by the instrumentality of pain, it leads to all the several
degrees of vexation, injustice, cruelty, oppression, and
tyranny. It is, in truth, the grand source of all wickedness,
of all the evil which man brings upon man. When the
education is so deplorably bad as to allow an association to
be formed in the mind of the child between the grand object
of desire, the command over the wills of other men, and
the fears and pains of other men, as the means; the foundation is laid of the bad character,—the bad son, the bad
brother, the bad husband, the bad father, the bad neighbour,
the bad magistrate, the bad citizen,—to sum up all in one

word, the bad man. Yet, true, it is, a great part of education
is still so conducted as to form that association. The child,
while it yet hangs at the breast, is often allowed to find out
by experience, that crying, and the annoyance which it
gives, is that by which chiefly it can command the services
of its nurse, and obtain the pleasures which it desires. There
is not one child in fifty, who has not learned to make its
cries and wailings an instrument of power; very often they
are an instrument of absolute tyranny. When the evil grows
to excess, the vulgar say the child is spoiled. Not only is the
child allowed to exert an influence over the wills of others,
by means of their pains; it finds, that frequently, sometimes
most frequently, its own will is needlessly and unduly com-
manded by the same means, pain, and the fear of pain. All
these sensations concur in establishing a firm association
between the idea of the grand object of desire, command
over the acts of other men, and the idea of pain and terror,
as the means of acquiring it. That those who have been
subject to tyranny, are almost always desirous of being
tyrants in their turn; that is to say, that a strong association
has been formed in their minds, between the ideas of
pleasure and dignity, on the one hand, and those of the
exercise of tyranny, on the other, is a matter of old and
invariable observation. An anecdote has just been mentioned to us, so much in point, that we will repeat it, as
resting on its own probability, though it is hearsay evidence
(very good, however, of its kind) on which we have received
it. At Eton, in consequence, it is probable, of the criticisms
which the press has usefully made upon the system of *fagging*
(as it is called), at the public schools, a proposition was lately
made, among the boys themselves, for abolishing it. The
idea originated with the elder boys, who were in possession
of the power; a power of a very unlimited and formidable
description; and by them was warmly supported. It was,

however, opposed with still greater vehemence by the junior boys, the boys who were then the victims of it. The expected pleasure of tyrannizing in their turn, outweighed the pain of their present slavery. In this case, too, as in most others, the sources of those trains which govern us are two—the impressions made upon ourselves, and the trains which we copy from others. Besides the impressions just recounted, if the trains which pass in the minds of those by whom the child is surrounded, and which he is made to conceive by means of their words, and other signs, lead constantly from the idea of command over the wills of other men, as the grand object of desire, to the ideas of pain and terror as the means, the repetition of the copied trains increases the effect of the native impressions, and establishes and confirms the maleficent character. These are the few things we can afford to adduce upon the subject of Domestic Education.

2. In the next place comes that which we have denominated TECHNICAL EDUCATION. To this the term Education has been commonly confined; or, rather, the word Education has been used in a sense so unhappily restricted, that it has extended only to a part of that which we call Technical Education. It has not extended to all the arts, but only to those which have been denominated liberal.

The question here occurs—What is the sort of education required for the different classes of society, and what should be the difference in the training provided for each? Before we can treat explicitly of technical education, we must endeavour to show, in what manner, at least, this question ought to be resolved.

There are certain qualities, the possession of which is desirable in all classes. There are certain qualities, the possession of which is desirable in some, not in others. As far as those qualities extend which ought to be common to all, there ought to be a correspondent training for all. It is only in respect to those qualities which are not desirable in all, that a difference in the mode of training is required.

What then are the qualities, the possession of which is desirable in all? They are the qualities which we have already named as chiefly subservient to the happiness of the individual himself, and of other men; Intelligence, Temperance, and Benevolence. It is very evident that these qualities are desirable in all men; and if it were possible to get them all in the highest possible degree in all men, so much the more would human nature be exalted.

The chief difficulty respects Intelligence; for it will be readily allowed, that almost equal care ought to be taken, in all classes, of the trains leading to the settled dispositions which the terms Temperance and Benevolence denote. Benevolence, as we have above described it, can hardly be said to be of more importance to the happiness of man in one class than in another. If we bear in mind, also, the radical meaning of Temperance, that it is the steady habit of resisting a present desire, for the sake of a greater good, we shall readily grant, that it is not less necessary to happiness in one rank of life than in another. It is only necessary to see, that temperance, though always the same disposition, is not always exerted on the same objects, in the different conditions of life. It is no demand of temperance, in the man who can afford it, to deny himself animal food; it may be an act of temperance in the man whose harder circumstances require that he should limit himself to coarser fare. It is also true, that the trains which lead to Temperance and Benevolence may be equally cultivated in all classes. The impressions which persons are made to receive, and the trains of others which they are made to copy, may, with equal certainty, be guided to the generating of those two qualities in all the different classes of society. We deem it

unnecessary, (here indeed, it is impossible) to enter into
the details of what may be done in the course of technical
education, to generate, or to confirm, the dispositions of
Temperance and Benevolence. It can be nothing more
than the application of the principles which we developed,
when we endeavoured to show in what manner the circumstances of domestic education might be employed for generating the trains on which these mental qualities depend.

Technical Education, we shall then consider, as having
chiefly to do with *Intelligence*.

The first question, as we have said before, respects what
is desirable for all,—the second, what is desirable for each
of the several classes. Till recently, it was denied, that intelligence was a desirable quality in the great body of the
people; and as intelligence is power, such is an unavoidable
opinion in the breasts of those who think that the human
race ought to consist of two classes,—one that of the op-
pressors, another that of the oppressed. The concern which
is now felt for the education of the working classes, shows
that we have made a great step in knowledge, and in that
genuine morality which ever attends it.

The analysis of the ideas decides the whole matter at
once. If education be to communicate the art of happiness;
and if intelligence consists of two parts, a knowledge of the
order of those events of nature on which our pleasures and
pains depend, and the sagacity which discovers the best
means for the attaining of ends; the question, whether the
people should be educated, is the same with the question,
whether they should be happy or miserable. The question,
whether they should have more or less of intelligence, is
merely the question, whether they should have more or less
of misery, when happiness might be given in its stead. It
has been urged that men are, by daily experience, evinced
not to be happy, not to be moral, in proportion to their

knowledge. It is a shallow objection. Long ago it was observed by Hume, that knowledge and its accompaniments, morality and happiness, may not be strictly conjoined in every individual, but that they are infallibly so in every age, and in every country. The reason is plain; a natural cause may be hindered of its operation in one particular instance, though in a great variety of instances it is sure to prevail. Besides, there may be a good deal of knowledge in an individual, but not knowledge of the best things; this cannot easily happen in a whole people; neither the whole nor the greater part will miss the right objects of knowledge, when knowledge is generally diffused.

As evidence of the vast progress which we have made in right thinking upon this subject, we cannot help remarking, that even Milton and Locke, though both men of great benevolence toward the larger family of mankind, and both men whose sentiments were democratical, yet seem, in their writings on education, to have had in view no education but that of the *gentleman*. It had not presented itself, even to their minds, that education was a blessing in which the indigent orders could be made to partake.

As we strive for an equal degree of justice, an equal degree of temperance, an equal degree of veracity, in the poor as in the rich, so ought we to strive for an equal degree of intelligence, if there were not a preventing cause. It is absolutely necessary for the existence of the human race, that labour should be performed, that food should be produced, and other things provided, which human welfare requires. A large proportion of mankind is required for this labour. Now, then, in regard to all this portion of mankind, that labours, only such a portion of time can by them be given to the acquisition of intelligence, as can be abstracted from labour. The difference between intelligence and the other qualities desirable in the mind of man, is this,

That much of time, exclusively devoted to the fixing of the associations on which the other qualities depend is not necessary; such trains may go on while other things are attended to, and amid the whole of the business of life. The case is to a certain extent, the same with intelligence; but, to a great extent, it is not. Time must be exclusively devoted to the acquisition of it; and there are degrees of command over knowledge to which the whole period of human life is not more than sufficient. There are degrees, therefore, of intelligence, which must be reserved to those who are not obliged to labour.

The question is (and it is a question which none can exceed in importance), What is the degree attainable by the most numerous class? To this we have no doubt, it will, in time, very clearly appear, that a most consolatory answer may be given. We have no doubt it will appear that a very high degree is attainable by them. It is now almost universally acknowledged, that, on all conceivable accounts, it is desirable that the great body of the people should not be wretchedly poor; that when the people are wretchedly poor, all classes are vicious, all are hateful, and all are unhappy. If so far raised above wretched poverty, as to be capable of being virtuous; though it be still necessary for them to earn their bread by the sweat of their brow, they are not bound down to such incessant toil as to have no time for the acquisition of knowledge, and the exercise of intellect. Above all, a certain portion of the first years of life are admirably available to this great end. With a view to the productive powers of their very labour, it is desirable that the animal frame should not be devoted to it before a certain age, before it has approached the point of maturity. This holds in regard to the lower animals; a horse is less valuable, less, in regard to that very labour for which he is valuable at all, if he is forced upon it too soon. There is an actual loss, therefore, even in productive powers, even in good economy, and in the way of health and strength, if the young of the human species are bound close to labour before they are fifteen or sixteen years of age. But if those years are skilfully employed in the acquisition of knowledge, in rendering all those trains habitual on which intelligence depends, it may be easily shown that a very high degree of intellectual acquirements may be gained; that a firm foundation may be laid for a life of mental action, a life of wisdom, and reflection, and ingenuity, even in those by whom the most ordinary labour will fall to be performed. In proof of this, we may state, that certain individuals in London, a few years ago, some of them men of great consideration among their countrymen, devised a plan for filling up those years with useful instruction; a plan which left the elements of hardly any branch of knowledge unprovided for; and at an expense which would exceed the means of no class of a population, raised as much above wretched poverty as all men profess to regard as desirable. Mr. Bentham called this plan of instruction by the Greek name *Chrestomathia*; and developed his own ideas of the objects and mode of instruction, with that depth and comprehension which belong to him, in a work which he published under that name.* Of the practicability of the scheme no competent judge has ever doubted; and the difficulty of collecting funds is the only reason why it has not been demonstrated by experiment, how much of that intelligence which is desirable for all may be communicated to all.†

* *Chrestomathia*, being a collection of papers, explanatory of the design of an institution proposed to be set on foot, under the name of Chrestomathic day school, &c. By Jeremy Bentham, Esq.

† We mention with extraordinary satisfaction, that an idea of education, hardly less extensive than what is here alluded to, has been adopted by that enlightened and indefatigable class of men, the Baptist

Beside the knowledge of faculties, which all classes
should possess in common, there are branches of knowledge

Missionaries in India, for the population, poor as well as ignorant,
of those extensive and populous regions. A small volume, entitled
*Hints relative to Native Schools, together with the Outline of an Insti-
tution for their Extension and Management,* was printed at the mission
press at Serampore in 1816; and, as it cannot come into the hands of
many of our readers, we gladly copy from it the following passage,
in hopes that the example may be persuasive with many of our countrymen at home.

"It is true, that when these helps are provided, namely, a correct
system of orthography, a sketch of grammar, a simplified system of
arithmetic, and an extended vocabulary, little is done beyond laying
the foundation. Still, however, this foundation must be laid, if any
superstructure of knowledge and virtue be attempted relative to the
inhabitants of India. Yet, were the plan to stop here, something would
have been done. A peasant or an artificer, thus rendered capable of
writing as well as reading his own language with propriety, and made
acquainted with the principles of arithmetic, would be less liable to
become a prey to fraud among his own countrymen; and far better
able to claim for himself that protection from oppression which it is
the desire of every enlightened government to grant. But the chief
advantage derivable from this plan is, its facilitating the reception of
ideas which may enlarge and bless the mind in a high degree,—ideas
for which India must be indebted to the West, at present the seat of
science, and for the communication of which, generations yet unborn,
will pour benedictions on the British name.

"1. To this, then, might be added a concise, but perspicuous
account of the solar system, preceded by so much of the laws of
motion, of attraction, and gravity, as might be necessary to render
the solar system plain and intelligible. These ideas, however, should
not be communicated in the form of a treatise, but in that of simple
axioms, delivered in short and perspicuous sentences. This method
comes recommended by several considerations;—it agrees with the
mode in which doctrines are communicated in the *Hindoo Shastras,*
and is therefore congenial with the ideas of even the learned among
them; it would admit of these sentences being written from dictation,
and even committed to memory with advantage, as well as of their
being easily retained; and, finally, the conciseness of this method
would allow of a multitude of truths and facts relative to astronomy,
geography, and the principal phenomena of nature, being brought
before youth within a very small compass.

"2. This abstract of the solar system might be followed by a com-
pendious view of geography on the same plan—that of comprising
every particular in concise but luminous sentences. In this part it
would be proper to describe Europe particularly, because of its

and art, which they cannot all acquire, and, in respect to which, education must undergo a corresponding variety.

importance in the present state of the world; and Britain might, with propriety, be allowed to occupy in the compendium, that pre-eminence among the nations which the God of Providence has given her.

"3. To these might be added a number of popular truths and facts relative to natural philosophy. In the present improved state of knowledge, a thousand things have been ascertained relative to light, heat, air, water, to meteorology, mineralogy, chemistry, and natural history, of which the ancients had but a partial knowledge, and of which the natives of the East have as yet scarcely the faintest idea. These facts, now so clearly ascertained, could be conveyed in a very short compass of language, although the process of reasoning, which enables the mind to account for them, occupies many volumes. A knowledge of the facts themselves, however, would be almost invaluable to the Hindoos, as these facts would rectify and enlarge their ideas of the various objects of nature around them; and while they, in general, delighted as well as informed those who read them, they might inflame a few minds of a superior order with an unquenchable desire to know *why* these things are so, and thus urge them to those studies, which in Europe have led to the discovery of these important facts.

"4. To this view of the solar system of the earth, and the various objects it contains, might, with great advantage, be added such a compendium of history and chronology united, as should bring them acquainted with the state of the world in past ages, and with the principal events which have occurred since the creation of the world. With the creation it should commence, describe the primitive state of man, the entrance of evil, the corruption of the antediluvian age, the flood, and the peopling of the earth anew from one family, in which the compiler should avail himself of all the light thrown on this subject by modern research and investigation; he should particularly notice the nations of the east, incorporating, in their proper place, the best accounts we now have both of India and China. He should go on to notice the call of Abraham, the giving of the decalogue, the gradual revelations of the Scriptures of Truth, the settlement of Greece, its mythology, the Trojan war, the four great monarchies, the advent of the Saviour of men, the persecutions of the Christian church, the rise of Mahometanism, the origin of the papacy, the invention of printing, of gunpowder, and the mariner's compass, the reformation, the discovery of the passage to India by sea, and the various discoveries of modern science. Such a synopsis of history and chronology, composed on the same plan, that of comprising each event in a concise but perspicuous sentence, would exceedingly enlarge their ideas relative to the state of the world, certainly not to the disadvantage of Britain, whom God has now so exalted as to render her almost the arbitress of nations.

"5. Lastly, It would be highly proper to impart to them just ideas

The apprenticeships, for example, which youths are accustomed to serve to the useful arts, we regard as a branch of their education. Whether these apprenticeships, as they have hitherto been managed, have been good instruments of education, is a question of importance, about which there is now, among enlightened men, hardly any diversity of opinion. When the legislature undertakes to do for every man, what every man has abundant motives to do for himself, and better means than the legislature; the legislature takes a very unnecessary, commonly a not very innocent trouble. Into the details, however, of the best mode of teaching, to the working people, the arts by which the different commodities useful or agreeable to man are provided, we cannot possibly enter. We must content ourselves with marking it out as a distinct branch of the subject, and an important object of study.

With respect to the education of that class of society who have wealth and time for the acquisition of the highest measure of intelligence, there is one question to which every body must be prepared with an answer. If it be asked, whether, in the constitution of any establishment for the education of this class; call it university, call it college,

of themselves, relative both to body and mind, and to a future state of existence, by what may be termed a Compendium of Ethics and Morality. The complete absence of all just ideas of this kind, is the chief cause of that degradation of public morals so evident in this country.

"These various compendiums, after being written from dictation, in the manner described in the next section, might also furnish matter for reading; and when it is considered that, in addition to the sketch of grammar, the vocabulary, and the system of arithmetic, they include a view of the solar system, a synopsis of geography, a collection of facts relative to natural objects, an abstract of general history, and a compendium of ethics and morality, they will be found to furnish sufficient matter for reading while youth are at school."

Why should not the same idea be pursued in England, and as much knowledge conveyed to the youth of all classes at school, as the knowledge of the age, and the allotted period of schooling will admit?

school, or any thing else; there ought to be a provision for perpetual improvement; a provision to make the institution keep pace with the human mind; or whether, on the other hand, it ought to be so constituted as that there should not only be no provision for, but a strong spirit of resistance to, all improvement, a passion of adherence to whatever was established in a dark age, and a principle of hatred to those by whom improvement should be proposed; all indifferent men will pronounce, that such institution would be a curse rather than a blessing. That he is a *progressive* being, is the grand distinction of Man. He is the only progressive being upon this globe. When he is the most rapidly progressive, then he most completely fulfils his destiny. An institution for *education* which is hostile to progression, is, therefore, the most preposterous, and vicious thing, which the mind of man can conceive.

There are several causes which tend to impair the utility of old and opulent establishments for education. Their love of ease makes them love easy things, if they can derive from them as much credit, as they would from others which are more difficult. They endeavour, therefore, to give an artificial value to trifles. Old practices, which have become a hackneyed routine, are commonly easier than improvements; accordingly, they oppose improvements, even when it happens that they have no other interest in the preservation of abuses. Hardly is there a part of Europe in which the universities are not recorded in the annals of education, as the enemies of all innovation. "A peine la compagnie de Jésus," says d'Alembert, "commença-t-elle à se montrer en France, qu'elle essuya des difficultés sans nombre pour s'y établir. Les universités surtout firent les plus grands efforts, pour écarter ces nouveaux venus. Les Jésuites s'annonçaient pour enseigner gratuitement, ils comptoient déjà parmi eux des hommes savans et célèbres, supérieurs peut être à ceux dont les universités pouvaient se glorifier; l'intérêt et la vanité pouvaient donc suffire à leurs adversaires pour chercher à les exclure. On se rappelle les contradictions semblables que les ordres mendians essuyèrent de ces mêmes universités quand ils voulurent s'y introduire; contradictions fondées à peu près sur les mêmes motifs." (*Destruction des Jésuites en France*.) The celebrated German philosopher, Wolf, remarks the aversion of the universities to all improvement, as a notorious fact, derived from adequate motives: "Non adeo impune turbare licet scholarium quietem, et docentibus lucrosam, et discentibus jucundam."—(Wolfii *Logica*, Dedic. p. 2.)

But though such and so great are the evil tendencies which are to be guarded against in associated seminaries of education; evil tendencies which are apt to be indefinitely increased, when they are united with an ecclesiastical establishment, because, whatever the vices of the ecclesiastical system, the universities have in that case an interest to bend the whole of their force to the support of those vices, and to that end to vitiate the human mind, which can only be rendered the friend of abuses in proportion as it is vitiated intellectually, or morally, or both; it must, notwithstanding, be confessed, that there are great advantages in putting it in the power of the youth to obtain all the branches of their education in one place; even in assembling a certain number of them together, when the principle of emulation acts with powerful effect; and in carrying on the complicated process according to a regular plan, under a certain degree of discipline, and with the powerful spur of publicity. All this ought not to be rashly sacrificed; nor does there appear to be any insuperable difficulty, in devising a plan for the attainment of all those advantages, without the evils which have more or less adhered to all the collegiate establishments which Europe has yet enjoyed.

After the consideration of these questions, we ought next to describe, and prove by analysis, the exercises which would be most conducive in forming those virtues which we include under the name of intelligence. But it is very evident, that this is a matter of detail far too extensive for so limited a design as ours. And though, in common language, Education means hardly any thing more than making the youth perform those exercises; and a treatise on Education means little more than an account of them; we must content ourselves with marking the place which the inquiry would occupy in a complete system, and proceed to offer a few remarks on the two remaining branches of the subject, *Social Education*, and *Political Education*.

The branches of moral education, heretofore spoken of, operate upon the individual in the first period of life, and when he is not as yet his own master. The two just now mentioned operate upon the whole period of life, but more directly and powerfully after the technical education is at an end, and the youth is launched into the world under his own control.

3. SOCIAL EDUCATION is that in which Society is the Institutor. That the Society in which an individual moves produces great effects upon his mode of thinking and acting, every body knows by indubitable experience. The object is, to ascertain the extent of this influence, the mode in which it is brought about, and hence the means of making it operate in a good, rather than an evil direction.

The force of this influence springs from two sources: the principle of imitation; and the power of the society over our happiness and misery.

We have already shown, that when, by means of words and other signs of what is passing in the minds of other men, we are made to conceive, step by step, the trains which are governing them, those trains, by repetition, become habitual to our own minds, and exert the same influence over us as those which arise from our own impressions. It is very evident, that those trains which are most habitually passing in the minds of all those individuals by whom we are surrounded, must be made to pass with extraordinary frequency through our own minds, and must, unless where extraordinary means are used to prevent them from producing their natural effect, engross to a proportional degree the dominion of our minds. With this slight indication of this source of the power which society usurps over our minds, that is, of the share which it has in our education, we must content ourselves, and pass to the next.

Nothing is more remarkable in human nature, than the intense desire which we feel of the favourable regards of mankind. Few men could bear to live under an exclusion from the breast of every human being. It is astonishing how great a portion of all the actions of men are directed to these favourable regards, and to no other object. The greatest princes, the most despotical masters of human destiny, when asked what they aim at by their wars and conquests, would answer, if sincere, as Frederic of Prussia answered, *pour faire parler de soi*; to occupy a large space in the admiration of mankind. What are the ordinary pursuits of wealth and of power, which kindle to such a height the ardour of mankind? Not the mere love of eating and of drinking, or all the physical objects together, which wealth can purchase or power command. With these every man is in the long run speedily satisfied. It is the easy command, which those advantages procure over the favourable regards of society,—it is this which renders the desire of wealth unbounded, and gives it that irresistible influence which it possesses in directing the human mind.

Whatever, then, are the trains of thought, whatever is the course of action which most strongly recommends us to the favourable regards of those among whom we live, these we feel the strongest motive to cultivate and display; whatever trains of thought and course of action expose us to their unfavourable regards, these we feel the strongest motives to avoid. These inducements, operating upon us continually, have an irresistible influence in creating habits, and in moulding, that is, educating us, into a character conformable to the society in which we move. This is the general principle; it might be illustrated in detail by many of the most interesting and instructive phenomena of human life; it is an illustration, however, which we cannot pursue.

To what extent the habits and character, which those influences tend to produce, may engross the man, will no doubt depend, to a certain degree, upon the powers of the domestic and technical education which he has undergone. We may conceive that certain trains might, by the skilful employment of the early years, be rendered so habitual as to be uncontrollable by any habits which the subsequent period of life could induce, and that those trains might be the decisive ones, on which intelligent and moral conduct depends. The influence of a vicious and ignorant society would in this case be greatly reduced; but still, the actual rewards and punishments which society has to bestow, upon those who please, and those who displease it; the good and evil, which it gives, or withholds, are so great, that to adopt the opinions which it approves, to perform the acts which it admires, to acquire the character, in short, which it "delighteth to honour," can seldom fail to be the leading object of those of whom it is composed. And as this potent influence operates upon those who conduct both the domestic education and the technical, it is next to impossible that the trains which are generated, even during the time of their operation, should not fall in with, instead of counteracting, the trains which the social education produces; it is next to impossible, therefore, that the whole man should not take the shape which that influence is calculated to impress upon him.

4. The POLITICAL EDUCATION is the last, which we have undertaken to notice, of the agents employed in forming the character of man. The importance of this subject has not escaped observation. Some writers have treated of it in a comprehensive and systematical manner. And a still greater number have illustrated it by occasional and striking remarks. It is, nevertheless, true, that the full and perfect exposition of it yet remains to be made.

The Political Education is like the key-stone of the arch; the strength of the whole depends upon it. We have seen that the strength of the Domestic and the Technical Education depends almost entirely upon the Social. Now it is certain, that the nature of the Social depends almost entirely upon the Political; and the most important part of the Physical (that which operates with greatest force upon the greatest number, the state of aliment and labour of the lower classes), is, in the long-run, determined by the action of the political machine. The play, therefore, of the political machine acts immediately upon the mind, and with extraordinary power; but this is not all; it also acts upon almost every thing else by which the character of the mind is apt to be formed.

It is a common observation, that such as is the direction given to the desires and passions of men, such is the character of the men. The direction is given to the desires and passions of men by one thing, and one alone; the means by which the grand objects of desire may be attained. Now this is certain, that the means by which the grand objects of desire may be attained, depend almost wholly upon the political machine. When the political machine is such, that the grand objects of desire are seen to be the natural prizes of great and virtuous conduct—of high services to mankind, and of the generous and amiable sentiments from which great endeavours in the service of mankind naturally proceed—it is natural to see diffused among mankind a generous ardour in the acquisition of all those admirable qualities which prepare a man for admirable actions; great intelligence, perfect self-command, and over-ruling benevolence. When the political machine is such that the grand objects of desire are seen to be the reward, not of virtue, not of talent, but of subservience to the will, and command over the affections of the ruling few; interest with the *man above* to be the only sure means to the next step in wealth, or power, or consideration, and so on; the means of pleasing the man above become, in that case, the great object of pursuit. And as the favours of the man above are necessarily limited—as some, therefore, of the candidates for his favour can only obtain the objects of their desire by disappointing others—the arts of supplanting rise into importance; and the whole of that tribe of faculties denoted by the words intrigue, flattery, back-biting, treachery, &c., are the fruitful offspring of that political education which government, where the interests of the subject many are but a secondary object, cannot fail to produce.

II

EXTRACTS FROM JOHN STUART MILL'S AUTOBIOGRAPHY

I

CHILDHOOD & EARLY EDUCATION

It seems proper that I should prefix to the following bio-graphical sketch, some mention of the reasons which have made me think it desirable that I should leave behind me such a memorial of so uneventful a life as mine. I do not for a moment imagine that any part of what I have to relate, can be interesting to the public as a narrative, or as being connected with myself. But I have thought that in an age in which education, and its improvement, are the subject of more, if not of profounder study than at any former period of English history, it may be useful that there should be some record of an education which was unusual and remarkable, and which, whatever else it may have done, has proved how much more than is commonly supposed may be taught, and well taught, in those early years which, in the common modes of what is called instruction, are little better than wasted. It has also seemed to me that in an age of transition in opinions, there may be somewhat both of interest and of benefit in noting the successive phases of any mind which was always pressing forward, equally ready to learn and to unlearn either from its own thoughts or from those of others. But a motive which weighs more with me than either of these, is a desire to make acknow-ledgment of the debts which my intellectual and moral development owes to other persons; some of them of recognised eminence, others less known than they deserve to be, and the one to whom most of all is due, one whom the world had no opportunity of knowing. The reader whom these things do not interest, has only himself to blame if he reads farther, and I do not desire any other indulgence from him than that of bearing in mind, that for him these pages were not written.

I was born in London, on the 20th of May, 1806, and was the eldest son of James Mill, the author of the *History of British India*. My father, the son of a petty tradesman and (I believe) small farmer, at Northwater Bridge, in the county of Angus, was, when a boy, recommended by his abilities to the notice of Sir John Stuart, of Fettercairn, one of the Barons of the Exchequer in Scotland, and was, in consequence, sent to the University of Edinburgh, at the expense of a fund established by Lady Jane Stuart (the wife of Sir John Stuart) and some other ladies for educating young men for the Scottish Church. He there went through the usual course of study, and was licensed as a Preacher, but never followed the profession; having satisfied himself that he could not believe the doctrines of that or any other Church. For a few years he was a private tutor in various families in Scotland, among others that of the Marquis of Tweeddale, but ended by taking up his residence in London, and devoting himself to authorship. Nor had he any other means of support until 1819, when he obtained an appointment in the India House.

In this period of my father's life there are two things which it is impossible not to be struck with: one of them unfortunately a very common circumstance, the other a most uncommon one. The first is, that in his position, with no resource but the precarious one of writing in periodicals, he married and had a large family; conduct than which nothing could be more opposed, both as a matter of good sense and of duty, to the opinions which, at least at a later period of life, he strenuously upheld. The other circumstance, is the extraordinary energy which was required to lead the life he led, with the disadvantages under which he laboured from the first, and with those which he brought upon himself by his marriage. It would have been no small thing, had he done no more than to support himself and his family during so many years by writing, without ever being in debt, or in any pecuniary difficulty; holding, as he did, opinions, both in politics and in religion, which were more odious to all persons of influence, and to the common run of prosperous Englishmen in that generation than either before or since; and being not only a man whom nothing would have induced to write against his convictions, but one who invariably threw into everything he wrote, as much of his convictions as he thought the circumstances would in any way permit: being, it must also be said, one who never did anything negligently; never undertook any task, literary or other, on which he did not conscientiously bestow all the labour necessary for performing it adequately. But he, with these burdens on him, planned, commenced, and completed, the *History of India*; and this in the course of about ten years, a shorter time than has been occupied (even by writers who had no other employment) in the production of almost any other historical work of equal bulk, and of anything approaching to the same amount of reading and research. And to this is to be added, that during the whole period, a considerable part of almost every day was employed in the instruction of his children: in the case of one of whom, myself, he exerted an amount of labour, care, and perseverance rarely, if ever, employed for a similar purpose, in endeavouring to give, according to his own conception, the highest order of intellectual education.

A man who, in his own practice, so vigorously acted up

to the principle of losing no time, was likely to adhere to the same rule in the instruction of his pupil. I have no remembrance of the time when I began to learn Greek, I have been told that it was when I was three years old. My earliest recollection on the subject, is that of committing to memory what my father termed vocables, being lists of common Greek words, with their signification in English, which he wrote out for me on cards. Of grammar, until some years later, I learnt no more than the inflexions of the nouns and verbs, but, after a course of vocables, proceeded at once to translation; and I faintly remember going through Æsop's *Fables*, the first Greek book which I read. The *Anabasis*, which I remember better, was the second. I learnt no Latin until my eighth year. At that time I had read, under my father's tuition, a number of Greek prose authors, among whom I remember the whole of Herodotus, and of Xenophon's *Cyropædia* and *Memorials of Socrates*; some of the lives of the philosophers by Diogenes Laertius; part of Lucian, and Isocrates *ad Demonicum* and *ad Nicoclem*. I also read, in 1813, the first six dialogues (in the common arrangement) of Plato, from the *Euthyphron* to the *Theætetus* inclusive: which last dialogue, I venture to think, would have been better omitted, as it was totally impossible I should understand it. But my father, in all his teaching, demanded of me not only the utmost that I could do, but much that I could by no possibility have done. What he was himself willing to undergo for the sake of my instruction, may be judged from the fact, that I went through the whole process of preparing my Greek lessons in the same room and at the same table at which he was writing: and as in those days Greek and English lexicons were not, and I could make no more use of a Greek and Latin lexicon than could be made without having yet begun to learn Latin, I was forced to have recourse to him for the meaning of every word which I did not know. This incessant interruption, he, one of the most impatient of men, submitted to, and wrote under that interruption several volumes of his *History* and all else that he had to write during those years.

The only thing besides Greek, that I learnt as a lesson in this part of my childhood, was arithmetic: this also my father taught me: it was the task of the evenings, and I well remember its disagreeableness. But the lessons were only a part of the daily instruction I received. Much of it consisted in the books I read by myself, and my father's discourses to me, chiefly during our walks. From 1810 to the end of 1813 we were living in Newington Green, then an almost rustic neighbourhood. My father's health required considerable and constant exercise, and he walked habitually before breakfast, generally in the green lanes towards Hornsey. In these walks I always accompanied him, and with my earliest recollections of green fields and wild flowers, is mingled that of the account I gave him daily of what I had read the day before. To the best of my remembrance, this was a voluntary rather than a prescribed exercise. I made notes on slips of paper while reading, and from these in the morning walks, I told the story to him; for the books were chiefly histories, of which I read in this manner a great number: Robertson's histories, Hume, Gibbon; but my greatest delight, then and for long afterwards, was Watson's *Philip the Second and Third*. The heroic defence of the Knights of Malta against the Turks, and of the revolted Provinces of the Netherlands against Spain, excited in me an intense and lasting interest. Next to Watson, my favourite historical reading was Hooke's *History of Rome*. Of Greece I had seen at that time no regular history, except school abridgments and the last two or three volumes of a translation of Rollin's *Ancient*

History, beginning with Philip of Macedon. But I read with great delight Langhorne's translation of Plutarch. In English history, beyond the time at which Hume leaves off, I remember reading Burnet's *History of his Own Time*, though I cared little for anything in it except the wars and battles; and the historical part of the *Annual Register*, from the beginning to about 1788, where the volumes my father borrowed for me from Mr. Bentham left off. I felt a lively interest in Frederic of Prussia during his difficulties, and in Paoli, the Corsican patriot; but when I came to the American war, I took my part, like a child as I was (until set right by my father) on the wrong side, because it was called the English side. In these frequent talks about the books I read, he used, as opportunity offered, to give me explanations and ideas respecting civilization, government, morality, mental cultivation, which he required me afterwards to restate to him in my own words. He also made me read, and give him a verbal account of, many books which would not have interested me sufficiently to induce me to read them of myself: among others, Millar's *Historical View of the English Government*, a book of great merit for its time, and which he highly valued; Mosheim's *Ecclesiastical History*, McCrie's *Life of John Knox*, and even Sewell and Rutty's Histories of the Quakers. He was fond of putting into my hands books which exhibited men of energy and resource in unusual circumstances, struggling against difficulties and overcoming them: of such works I remember Beaver's *African Memoranda*, and Collins's *Account of the First Settlement of New South Wales*. Two books which I never wearied of reading were Anson's *Voyages*, so delightful to most young persons, and a collection (Hawkesworth's, I believe) of *Voyages round the World*, in four volumes, beginning with Drake and ending with Cook and Bougainville. Of children's books, any more than of playthings, I had scarcely any, except an occasional gift from a relation or acquaintance: among those I had, *Robinson Crusoe* was preeminent, and continued to delight me through all my boyhood. It was no part, however, of my father's system to exclude books of amusement, though he allowed them very sparingly. Of such books he possessed at that time next to none, but he borrowed several for me; those which I remember are the *Arabian Nights*, Cazotte's *Arabian Tales*, *Don Quixote*, Miss Edgeworth's *Popular Tales*, and a book of some reputation in its day, Brooke's *Fool of Quality*.

In my eighth year I commenced learning Latin, in conjunction with a younger sister, to whom I taught it as I went on, and who afterwards repeated the lessons to my father: and from this time, other sisters and brothers being successively added as pupils, a considerable part of my day's work consisted of this preparatory teaching. It was a part which I greatly disliked; the more so, as I was held responsible for the lessons of my pupils, in almost as full a sense as for my own: I, however, derived from this discipline the great advantage, of learning more thoroughly and retaining more lastingly the things which I was set to teach: perhaps, too, the practice it afforded in explaining difficulties to others, may even at that age have been useful. In other respects, the experience of my boyhood is not favourable to the plan of teaching children by means of one another. The teaching, I am sure, is very inefficient as teaching, and I well know that the relation between teacher and taught is not a good moral discipline to either. I went in this manner through the Latin grammar, and a considerable part of Cornelius Nepos and Cæsar's *Commentaries*, but afterwards added to the superintendence of these lessons, much longer ones of my own.

In the same year in which I began Latin, I made my

first commencement in the Greek poets with the *Iliad.*
After I had made some progress in this, my father put
Pope's translation into my hands. It was the first English
verse I had cared to read, and it became one of the books
in which for many years I most delighted: I think I must
have read it from twenty to thirty times through. I should
not have thought it worth while to mention a taste appa-
rently so natural to boyhood, if I had not, as I think, observed that the keen enjoyment of this brilliant specimen
of narrative and versification is not so universal with boys,
as I should have expected both *à priori* and from my individual experience. Soon after this time I commenced
Euclid, and somewhat later, Algebra, still under my father's
tuition.

From my eighth to my twelfth year, the Latin books
which I remember reading were, the *Bucolics* of Virgil,
and the first six books of the *Æneid*; all Horace, except
the *Epodes*; the *Fables* of Phædrus; the first five books of
Livy (to which from my love of the subject I voluntarily
added, in my hours of leisure, the remainder of the first
decade); all Sallust; a considerable part of Ovid's *Meta-
morphoses*; some plays of Terence; two or three books of
Lucretius; several of the Orations of Cicero, and of his
writings on oratory; also his letters to Atticus, my father
taking the trouble to translate to me from the French the
historical explanations in Mingault's notes. In Greek I
read the *Iliad* and *Odyssey* through; one or two plays of
Sophocles, Euripides, and Aristophanes, though by these I
profited little; all Thucydides; the *Hellenics* of Xenophon;
a great part of Demosthenes, Æschines, and Lysias; Theo-
critus; Anacreon; part of the *Anthology*; a little of
Dionysius; several books of Polybius; and lastly Aristotle's
Rhetoric, which, as the first expressly scientific treatise on
any moral or psychological subject which I had read, and

containing many of the best observations of the ancients on human nature and life, my father made me study with peculiar care, and throw the matter of it into synoptic tables. During the same years I learnt elementary geometry and algebra thoroughly, the differential calculus, and other portions of the higher mathematics far from thoroughly: for my father, not having kept up this part of his early acquired knowledge, could not spare time to qualify himself for removing my difficulties, and left me to deal with them, with little other aid than that of books: while I was continually incurring his displeasure by my inability to solve difficult problems for which he did not see that I had not the necessary previous knowledge.

As to my private reading, I can only speak of what I remember. History continued to be my strongest predilection, and most of all ancient history. Mitford's *Greece* I read continually; my father had put me on my guard against the Tory prejudices of this writer, and his perversions of facts for the whitewashing of despots, and blackening of popular institutions. These points he discoursed on, exemplifying them from the Greek orators and historians, with such effect that in reading Mitford my sympathies were always on the contrary side to those of the author, and I could, to some extent, have argued the point against him: yet this did not diminish the ever new pleasure with which I read the book. Roman history, both in my old favourite, Hooke, and in Ferguson, continued to delight me. A book which, in spite of what is called the dryness of its style, I took great pleasure in, was the *Ancient Universal History*, through the incessant reading of which, I had my head full of historical details concerning the obscurest ancient people, while about modern history, except detached passages, such as the Dutch War of Independence, I knew and cared comparatively little. A voluntary exercise, to which throughout my boyhood I was much addicted, was what I called writing histories. I successively composed a Roman History, picked out of Hooke; an Abridgment of the *Ancient Universal History*; a History of Holland, from my favourite Watson and from an anonymous compilation; and in my eleventh and twelfth year I occupied myself with writing what I flattered myself was something serious. This was no less than a History of the Roman Government, compiled (with the assistance of Hooke) from Livy and Dionysius: of which I wrote as much as would have made an octavo volume, extending to the epoch of the Licinian Laws. It was, in fact, an account of the struggles between the patricians and plebeians, which now engrossed all the interest in my mind which I had previously felt in the mere wars and conquests of the Romans. I discussed all the constitutional points as they arose: though quite ignorant of Niebuhr's researches, I, by such lights as my father had given me, vindicated the Agrarian Laws on the evidence of Livy, and upheld, to the best of my ability, the Roman Democratic party. A few years later, in my contempt of my childish efforts, I destroyed all these papers, not then anticipating that I could ever feel any curiosity about my first attempts at writing and reasoning. My father encouraged me in this useful amusement, though, as I think judiciously, he never asked to see what I wrote; so that I did not feel that in writing it I was accountable to any one, nor had the chilling sensation of being under a critical eye.

But though these exercises in history were never a compulsory lesson, there was another kind of composition which was so, namely, writing verses, and it was one of the most disagreeable of my tasks. Greek and Latin verses I did not write, nor learnt the prosody of those languages. My father, thinking this not worth the time it required, contented himself with making me read aloud to him, and correcting false quantities. I never composed at all in Greek, even in prose, and but little in Latin. Not that my father could be indifferent to the value of this practice, in giving a thorough knowledge of these languages, but because there really was not time for it. The verses I was required to write were English. When I first read Pope's Homer, I ambitiously attempted to compose something of the same kind, and achieved as much as one book of a continuation of the *Iliad*. There, probably, the spontaneous promptings of my poetical ambition would have stopped; but the exercise, begun from choice, was continued by command. Conformably to my father's usual practice of explaining to me, as far as possible, the reasons for what he required me to do, he gave me, for this, as I well remember, two reasons highly characteristic of him: one was, that some things could be expressed better and more forcibly in verse than in prose: this, he said, was a real advantage. The other was, that people in general attached more value to verse than it deserved, and the power of writing it, was, on this account, worth acquiring. He generally left me to choose my own subjects, which, as far as I remember, were mostly addresses to some mythological personage or allegorical abstraction; but he made me translate into English verse many of Horace's shorter poems: I also remember his giving me Thomson's *Winter* to read, and afterwards making me attempt (without book) to write something myself on the same subject. The verses I wrote were, of course, the merest rubbish, nor did I ever attain any facility of versification, but the practice may have been useful in making it easier for me, at a later period, to acquire readiness of expression.* I had read, up to this time, very little English

---

* In a subsequent stage of boyhood, when these exercises had ceased to be compulsory, like most youthful writers I wrote tragedies; under

poetry. Shakspeare my father had put into my hands, chiefly for the sake of the historical plays, from which, however, I went on to the others. My father never was a great admirer of Shakspeare, the English idolatry of whom he used to attack with some severity. He cared little for any English poetry except Milton (for whom he had the highest admiration), Goldsmith, Burns, and Gray's *Bard*, which he preferred to his *Elegy*: perhaps I may add Cowper and Beattie. He had some value for Spenser, and I remember his reading to me (unlike his usual practice of making me read to him), the first book of the *Fairie Queene*; but I took little pleasure in it. The poetry of the present century he saw scarcely any merit in, and I hardly became acquainted with any of it till I was grown up to manhood, except the metrical romances of Walter Scott, which I read at his recommendation and was intensely delighted with; as I always was with animated narrative. Dryden's Poems were among my father's books, and many of these he made me read, but I never cared for any of them except *Alexander's Feast*, which, as well as many of the songs in Walter Scott, I used to sing internally, to a music of my own: to some of the latter, indeed, I went so far as to compose airs, which I still remember. Cowper's short poems I read with some pleasure, but never got far into the longer ones; and nothing in the two volumes interested me like the prose account of his three hares. In my thirteenth year I met with Campbell's poems, among which *Lochiel*, *Hohenlinden*, *The Exile of Erin*, and some others, gave me sensations I had never before experienced from poetry. Here, too, I made nothing of the longer poems, except the striking opening of *Gertrude of*

the inspiration not so much of Shakspeare as of Joanna Baillie, whose *Constantine Paleologus* in particular appeared to me one of the most glorious of human compositions. I still think it one of the best dramas of the last two centuries.

Wyoming, which long kept its place in my feelings as the perfection of pathos.

During this part of my childhood, one of my greatest amusements was experimental science; in the theoretical, however, not the practical sense of the word; not trying experiments—a kind of discipline which I have often regretted not having had—nor even seeing, but merely reading about them. I never remember being so wrapt up in any book, as I was in Joyce's *Scientific Dialogues*; and I was rather recalcitrant to my father's criticisms of the bad reasoning respecting the first principles of physics, which abounds in the early part of that work. I devoured treatises on Chemistry, especially that of my father's early friend and schoolfellow, Dr. Thomson, for years before I attended a lecture or saw an experiment.

From about the age of twelve, I entered into another and more advanced stage in my course of instruction; in which the main object was no longer the aids and appliances of thought, but the thoughts themselves. This commenced with Logic, in which I began at once with the *Organon*, and read it to the Analytics inclusive, but profited little by the *Posterior Analytics*, which belong to a branch of speculation I was not yet ripe for. Contemporaneously with the *Organon*, my father made me read the whole or parts of several of the Latin treatises on the scholastic logic; giving each day to him, in our walks, a minute account of what I had read, and answering his numerous and searching questions. After this, I went in a similar manner, through the *Computatio sive Logica* of Hobbes, a work of a much higher order of thought than the books of the school logicians, and which he estimated very highly; in my own opinion beyond its merits, great as these are. It was his invariable practice, whatever studies he exacted from me, to make me as far as possible understand and feel the utility of them: and this he deemed peculiarly fitting in the case of the syllogistic logic, the usefulness of which had been impugned by so many writers of authority. I well remember how, and in what particular walk, in the neighbourhood of Bagshot Heath (where we were on a visit to his old friend Mr. Wallace, then one of the Mathematical Professors at Sandhurst) he first attempted by questions to make me think on the subject, and frame some conception of what constituted the utility of the syllogistic logic, and when I had failed in this, to make me understand it by explanations. The explanations did not make the matter at all clear to me at the time; but they were not therefore useless; they remained as a nucleus for my observations and reflections to crystallize upon; the import of his general remarks being interpreted to me, by the particular instances which came under my notice afterwards. My own consciousness and experience ultimately led me to appreciate quite as highly as he did, the value of an early practical familiarity with the school logic. I know of nothing, in my education, to which I think myself more indebted for whatever capacity of thinking I have attained. The first intellectual operation in which I arrived at any proficiency, was dissecting a bad argument, and finding in what part the fallacy lay: and though whatever capacity of this sort I attained, was due to the fact that it was an intellectual exercise in which I was most perseveringly drilled by my father, yet it is also true that the school logic, and the mental habits acquired in studying it, were among the principal instruments of this drilling. I am persuaded that nothing, in modern education, tends so much, when properly used, to form exact thinkers, who attach a precise meaning to words and propositions, and are not imposed on by vague, loose, or ambiguous terms. The boasted influence of mathematical studies is nothing to it; for in mathematical processes, none of the real difficulties of correct ratiocination occur. It is also a study peculiarly adapted to an early stage in the education of philosophical students, since it does not presuppose the slow process of acquiring, by experience and reflection, valuable thoughts of their own. They may become capable of disentangling the intricacies of confused and self-contradictory thought, before their own thinking faculties are much advanced; a power which, for want of some such discipline, many otherwise able men altogether lack; and when they have to answer opponents, only endeavour, by such arguments as they can command, to support the opposite conclusion, scarcely even attempting to confute the reasonings of their antagonists; and, therefore, at the utmost, leaving the question, as far as it depends on argument, a balanced one.

During this time, the Latin and Greek books which I continued to read with my father were chiefly such as were worth studying, not for the language merely, but also for the thoughts. This included much of the orators, and especially Demosthenes, some of whose principal orations I read several times over, and wrote out, by way of exercise, a full analysis of them. My father's comments on these orations when I read them to him were very instructive to me. He not only drew my attention to the insight they afforded into Athenian institutions, and the principles of legislation and government which they often illustrated, but pointed out the skill and art of the orator—how everything important to his purpose was said at the exact moment when he had brought the minds of his audience into the state most fitted to receive it; how he made steal into their minds, gradually and by insinuation, thoughts which, if expressed in a more direct manner would have roused their opposition. Most of these reflections were beyond my capacity of full comprehension at the time; but they left

seed behind, which germinated in due season. At this time
I also read the whole of Tacitus, Juvenal, and Quintilian.
The latter, owing to his obscure style and to the scholastic
details of which many parts of his treatise are made up, is
little read, and seldom sufficiently appreciated. His book
is a kind of encyclopædia of the thoughts of the ancients
on the whole field of education and culture; and I have
retained through life many valuable ideas which I can distinctly trace to my reading of him, even at that early age.
It was at this period that I read, for the first time, some of
the most important dialogues of Plato, in particular the
Gorgias, the *Protagoras*, and the *Republic*. There is no
author to whom my father thought himself more indebted
for his own mental culture, than Plato, or whom he more
frequently recommended to young students. I can bear
similar testimony in regard to myself. The Socratic method,
of which the Platonic dialogues are the chief example, is
unsurpassed as a discipline for correcting the errors, and
clearing up the confusions incident to the *intellectus sibi
permissus*, the understanding which has made up all its
bundles of associations under the guidance of popular
phraseology. The close, searching *elenchus* by which the
man of vague generalities is constrained either to express
his meaning to himself in definite terms, or to confess that
he does not know what he is talking about; the perpetual
testing of all general statements by particular instances;
the siege in form which is laid to the meaning of large
abstract terms, by fixing upon some still larger class-name
which includes that and more, and dividing down to the
thing sought—marking out its limits and definition by a
series of accurately drawn distinctions between it and each
of the cognate objects which are successively parted off
from it—all this, as an education for precise thinking, is
inestimable, and all this, even at that age, took such hold

of me that it became part of my own mind. I have felt
ever since that the title of Platonist belongs by far better
right to those who have been nourished in, and have endeavoured to practise Plato's mode of investigation, than
to those who are distinguished only by the adoption of
certain dogmatical conclusions, drawn mostly from the least
intelligible of his works, and which the character of his mind
and writings makes it uncertain whether he himself regarded as anything more than poetic fancies, or philosophic
conjectures.

In going through Plato and Demosthenes, since I could
now read these authors, as far as the language was concerned, with perfect ease, I was not required to construe
them sentence by sentence, but to read them aloud to my
father, answering questions when asked: but the particular
attention which he paid to elocution (in which his own
excellence was remarkable) made this reading aloud to him
a most painful task. Of all things which he required me to
do, there was none which I did so constantly ill, or in which
he so perpetually lost his temper with me. He had thought
much on the principles of the art of reading, especially the
most neglected part of it, the inflections of the voice, or
modulation as writers on elocution call it (in contrast with
articulation on the one side, and *expression* on the other),
and had reduced it to rules, grounded on the logical analysis
of a sentence. These rules he strongly impressed upon me,
and took me severely to task for every violation of them:
but I even then remarked (though I did not venture to
make the remark to him) that though he reproached me
when I read a sentence ill, and *told* me how I ought to have
read it, he never, by reading it himself, *showed* me how it
ought to be read. A defect running through his otherwise
admirable modes of instruction, as it did through all his
modes of thought, was that of trusting too much to the

intelligibleness of the abstract, when not embodied in the concrete. It was at a much later period of my youth, when practising elocution by myself, or with companions of my own age, that I for the first time understood the object of his rules, and saw the psychological grounds of them. At that time I and others followed out the subject into its ramifications and could have composed a very useful treatise, grounded on my father's principles. He himself left those principles and rules unwritten. I regret that when my mind was full of the subject, from systematic practice, I did not put them, and our improvements of them, into a formal shape.

A book which contributed largely to my education, in the best sense of the term, was my father's *History of India*. It was published in the beginning of 1818. During the year previous, while it was passing through the press, I used to read the proof sheets to him; or rather, I read the manuscript to him while he corrected the proofs. The number of new ideas which I received from this remarkable book, and the impulse and stimulus as well as guidance given to my thoughts by its criticisms and disquisitions on society and civilization in the Hindoo part, on institutions and the acts of governments in the English part, made my early familiarity with it eminently useful to my subsequent progress. And though I can perceive deficiencies in it now as compared with a perfect standard, I still think it, if not the most, one of the most instructive histories ever written, and one of the books from which most benefit may be derived by a mind in the course of making up its opinions.

The Preface, among the most characteristic of my father's writings, as well as the richest in materials of thought, gives a picture which may be entirely depended on, of the sentiments and expectations with which he wrote the *History*. Saturated as the book is with the opinions and modes of judgment of a democratic radicalism then regarded as extreme; and treating with a severity, at that time most unusual, the English Constitution, the English law, and all parties and classes who possessed any considerable influence in the country; he may have expected reputation, but certainly not advancement in life, from its publication; nor could he have supposed that it would raise up anything but enemies for him in powerful quarters: least of all could he have expected favour from the East India Company, to whose commercial privileges he was unqualifiedly hostile, and on the acts of whose government he had made so many severe comments: though, in various parts of his book, he bore a testimony in their favour, which he felt to be their just due, namely, that no Government had on the whole given so much proof, to the extent of its lights, of good intention towards its subjects; and that if the acts of any other Government had the light of publicity as completely let in upon them, they would, in all probability, still less bear scrutiny.

On learning, however, in the spring of 1819, about a year after the publication of the *History*, that the East India Directors desired to strengthen the part of their home establishment which was employed in carrying on the correspondence with India, my father declared himself a candidate for that employment, and, to the credit of the Directors, successfully. He was appointed one of the Assistants of the Examiner of India Correspondence; officers whose duty it was to prepare drafts of despatches to India, for consideration by the Directors, in the principal departments of administration. In this office, and in that of Examiner, which he subsequently attained, the influence which his talents, his reputation, and his decision of character gave him, with superiors who really desired the good government of India, enabled him to a great extent to throw into his drafts of despatches, and to carry through the ordeal of the Court of Directors and Board of Control, without having their force much weakened, his real opinions on Indian subjects. In his History he had set forth, for the first time, many of the true principles of Indian administration: and his despatches, following his History, did more than had ever been done before to promote the improvement of India, and teach Indian officials to understand their business. If a selection of them were published, they would, I am convinced, place his character as a practical statesman fully on a level with his eminence as a speculative writer.

This new employment of his time caused no relaxation in his attention to my education. It was in this same year, 1819, that he took me through a complete course of political economy. His loved and intimate friend, Ricardo, had shortly before published the book which formed so great an epoch in political economy; a book which never would have been published or written, but for the entreaty and strong encouragement of my father; for Ricardo, the most modest of men, though firmly convinced of the truth of his doctrines, deemed himself so little capable of doing them justice in exposition and expression, that he shrank from the idea of publicity. The same friendly encouragement induced Ricardo, a year or two later, to become a member of the House of Commons; where, during the few remaining years of his life, unhappily cut short in the full vigour of his intellect, he rendered so much service to his and my father's opinions both on political economy and on other subjects.

Though Ricardo's great work was already in print, no didactic treatise embodying its doctrines, in a manner fit for learners, had yet appeared. My father, therefore, commenced instructing me in the science by a sort of lectures, which he delivered to me in our walks. He expounded each day a portion of the subject, and I gave him next day a written account of it, which he made me rewrite over and over again until it was clear, precise, and tolerably complete. In this manner I went through the whole extent of the science; and the written outline of it which resulted from my daily *compte rendu*, served him afterwards as notes from which to write his *Elements of Political Economy.* After this I read Ricardo, giving an account daily of what I read, and discussing, in the best manner I could, the collateral points which offered themselves in our progress.

On Money, as the most intricate part of the subject, he made me read in the same manner Ricardo's admirable pamphlets, written during what was called the Bullion controversy; to these succeeded Adam Smith; and in this reading it was one of my father's main objects to make me apply to Smith's more superficial view of political economy, the superior lights of Ricardo, and detect what was fallacious in Smith's arguments, or erroneous in any of his conclusions. Such a mode of instruction was excellently calculated to form a thinker; but it required to be worked by a thinker, as close and vigorous as my father. The path was a thorny one, even to him, and I am sure it was so to me, notwithstanding the strong interest I took in the subject. He was often, and much beyond reason, provoked by my failures in cases where success could not have been expected; but in the main his method was right, and it succeeded. I do not believe that any scientific teaching ever was more thorough, or better fitted for training the faculties, than the mode in which logic and political economy were taught to me by my father. Striving, even in an exaggerated degree, to call forth the activity of my faculties, by making me find out everything for myself, he gave his explanations not before, but after, I had felt the full force of the difficulties; and not only gave me an accurate knowledge of these two great subjects, as far as they were then understood, but made me a thinker on both. I thought for myself almost from the first, and occasionally thought differently from him, though for a long time only on minor points and making his opinion the ultimate standard. At a later period I even occasionally convinced him, and altered his opinion on some points of detail: which I state to his honour, not my own. It at once exemplifies his perfect candour, and the real worth of his method of teaching.

At this point concluded what can properly be called my lessons: when I was about fourteen I left England for more than a year; and after my return, though my studies went on under my father's general direction, he was no longer my schoolmaster. I shall therefore pause here, and turn back to matters of a more general nature connected with the part of my life and education included in the preceding reminiscences.

In the course of instruction which I have partially re-traced, the point most superficially apparent is the great effort to give, during the years of childhood, an amount of knowledge in what are considered the higher branches of education, which is seldom acquired (if acquired at all) until the age of manhood. The result of the experiment shows the ease with which this may be done, and places in a strong light the wretched waste of so many precious years as are spent in acquiring the modicum of Latin and Greek commonly taught to schoolboys; a waste which has led so many educational reformers to entertain the ill-judged proposal of discarding these languages altogether from general education. If I had been by nature extremely quick of apprehension, or had possessed a very accurate and retentive memory, or were of a remarkably active and energetic character, the trial would not be conclusive; but in all these natural gifts I am rather below than above par; what I could do, could assuredly be done by any boy or girl of average capacity and healthy physical constitution: and if I have accomplished anything, I owe it, among other fortunate circumstances, to the fact that through the early training bestowed on me by my father, I started, I may fairly say, with an advantage of a quarter of a century over my contemporaries.

There was one cardinal point in this training, of which I have already given some indication, and which, more than anything else, was the cause of whatever good it effected. Most boys or youths who have had much knowledge drilled into them, have their mental capacities not strengthened, but overlaid by it. They are crammed with mere facts, and with the opinions or phrases of other people, and these are accepted as a substitute for the power to form opinions of their own: and thus the sons of eminent fathers, who have spared no pains in their education, so often grow up mere parroters of what they have learnt, incapable of using their minds except in the furrows traced for them. Mine, however, was not an education of cram. My father never permitted anything which I learnt to degenerate into a mere exercise of memory. He strove to make the understanding not only go along with every step of the teaching, but, if possible, precede it. Anything which could be found out by thinking I never was told, until I had exhausted my efforts to find it out for myself. As far as I can trust my remembrance, I acquitted myself very lamely in this department; my recollection of such matters is almost wholly of failures, hardly ever of success. It is true the failures were often in things in which success in so early a stage of my progress, was almost impossible. I remember at some time in my thirteenth year, on my happening to use the word idea, he asked me what an idea was; and expressed some displeasure at my ineffectual efforts to define the word: I recollect also his indignation at my using the common expression that something was true in theory but required correction in practice; and how, after making me vainly strive to define the word theory, he explained its meaning, and showed the fallacy of the vulgar form of speech which I had used; leaving me fully persuaded that in being unable to give a correct definition of Theory, and in speaking of it as something which might be at variance with practice, I had shown unparalleled ignorance. In this he seems, and perhaps was, very unreasonable; but I think, only in being angry at my failure. A pupil from whom nothing is ever demanded which he cannot do, never does all he can.

One of the evils most liable to attend on any sort of early proficiency, and which often fatally blights its promise, my father most anxiously guarded against. This was self-conceit. He kept me, with extreme vigilance, out of the way of hearing myself praised, or of being led to make self-flattering comparisons between myself and others. From his own intercourse with me I could derive none but a very humble opinion of myself; and the standard of comparison he always held up to me, was not what other people did, but what a man could and ought to do. He completely succeeded in preserving me from the sort of influences he so much dreaded. I was not at all aware that my attainments were anything unusual at my age. If I accidentally had my attention drawn to the fact that some other boy knew less than myself—which happened less often than might be imagined—I concluded, not that I knew much, but that he, for some reason or other, knew little, or that his knowledge was of a different kind from mine. My state of mind was not humility, but neither was it arrogance.

I never thought of saying to myself, I am, or I can do, so and so. I neither estimated myself highly nor lowly: I did not estimate myself at all. If I thought anything about myself, it was that I was rather backward in my studies, since I always found myself so, in comparison with what my father expected from me. I assert this with confidence, though it was not the impression of various persons who saw me in my childhood. They, as I have since found, thought me greatly and disagreeably self-conceited; probably because I was disputatious, and did not scruple to give direct contradictions to things which I heard said. I suppose I acquired this bad habit from having been encouraged in an unusual degree to talk on matters beyond my age, and with grown persons, while I never had inculcated on me the usual respect for them. My father did not correct this ill-breeding and impertinence, probably from not being aware of it, for I was always too much in awe of him to be otherwise than extremely subdued and quiet in his presence. Yet with all this I had no notion of any superiority in myself; and well was it for me that I had not. I remember the very place in Hyde Park where, in my fourteenth year, on the eve of leaving my father's house for a long absence, he told me that I should find, as I got acquainted with new people, that I had been taught many things which youths of my age did not commonly know; and that many persons would be disposed to talk to me of this, and to compliment me upon it. What other things he said on this topic I remember very imperfectly; but he wound up by saying, that whatever I knew more than others, could not be ascribed to any merit in me, but to the very unusual advantage which had fallen to my lot, of having a father who was able to teach me, and willing to give the necessary trouble and time; that it was no matter of praise to me, if I knew more than those who had not had a similar advantage, but the deepest disgrace to me if I did not. I have a distinct remembrance, that the suggestion thus for the first time made to me, that I knew more than other youths who were considered well educated, was to me a piece of information, to which, as to all other things which my father told me, I gave implicit credence, but which did not at all impress me as a personal matter. I felt no disposition to glorify myself upon the circumstance that there were other persons who did not know what I knew; nor had I ever flattered myself that my acquirements, whatever they might be, were any merit of mine: but, now when my attention was called to the subject, I felt that what my father had said respecting my peculiar advantages was exactly the truth and common sense of the matter, and it fixed my opinion and feeling from that time forward.

It is evident that this, among many other of the purposes of my father's scheme of education, could not have been accomplished if he had not carefully kept me from having any great amount of intercourse with other boys. He was earnestly bent upon my escaping not only the corrupting influence which boys exercise over boys, but the contagion of vulgar modes of thought and feeling; and for this he was willing that I should pay the price of inferiority in the accomplishments which schoolboys in all countries chiefly cultivate. The deficiencies in my education were principally in the things which boys learn from being turned out to shift for themselves, and from being brought together in large numbers. From temperance and much walking, I grew up healthy and hardy, though not muscular; but I could do no feats of skill or physical strength, and knew none of the ordinary bodily exercises. It was not that play, or time for it, was refused me. Though no holidays were allowed, lest the habit of work should be broken, and a taste for idleness acquired, I had ample leisure in every day to amuse myself; but as I had no boy companions, and the animal need of physical activity was satisfied by walking, my amusements, which were mostly solitary, were in general, of a quiet, if not a bookish turn, and gave little stimulus to any other kind even of mental activity than that which was already called forth by my studies: I consequently remained long, and in a less degree have always remained, inexpert in anything requiring manual dexterity; my mind, as well as my hands, did its work very lamely when it was applied, or ought to have been applied, to the practical details which, as they are the chief interest of life to the majority of men, are also the things in which whatever mental capacity they have, chiefly shows itself: I was constantly meriting reproof by inattention, inobservance, and general slackness of mind in matters of daily life. My father was the extreme opposite in these particulars: his senses and mental faculties were always on the alert; he carried decision and energy of character in his whole manner and into every action of life: and this, as much as his talents, contributed to the strong impression which he always made upon those with whom he came into personal contact. But the children of energetic parents, frequently grow up unenergetic, because they lean on their parents, and the parents are energetic for them. The education which my father gave me was in itself much more fitted for training me to *know* than to *do*. Not that he was unaware of my deficiencies; both as a boy and as a youth I was incessantly smarting under his severe admonitions on the subject. There was anything but insensibility or tolerance on his part towards such shortcomings: but, while he saved me from the demoralizing effects of school life, he made no effort to provide me with any sufficient substitute for its practicalizing influences. Whatever qualities he himself, probably, had acquired without difficulty or special training, he seems to have supposed that I ought to acquire as easily. He had not, I think, bestowed the same amount of thought and attention on this, as on most other branches of education; and here, as well in some other points of my tuition, he seems to have expected effects without causes.

II
MORAL INFLUENCES IN EARLY YOUTH.
MY FATHER'S CHARACTER AND OPINIONS

In my education, as in that of everyone, the moral influences, which are so much more important than all others, are also the most complicated, and the most difficult to specify with any approach to completeness. Without attempting the hopeless task of detailing the circumstances by which, in this respect, my early character may have been shaped, I shall confine myself to a few leading points, which form an indispensable part of any true account of my education.

I was brought up from the first without any religious belief, in the ordinary acceptation of the term. My father, educated in the creed of Scotch Presbyterianism, had by his own studies and reflections been early led to reject not only the belief in Revelation, but the foundations of what is commonly called Natural Religion. I have heard him say, that the turning point of his mind on the subject was reading Butler's *Analogy*. That work, of which he always continued to speak with respect, kept him, as he said, for some considerable time, a believer in the divine authority of Christianity; by proving to him, that whatever are the difficulties in believing that the Old and New Testaments proceed from, or record the acts of, a perfectly wise and good being, the same and still greater difficulties stand in the way of the belief, that a being of such a character can have been the Maker of the universe. He considered

Butler's argument as conclusive against the only opponents for whom it was intended. Those who admit an omnipotent as well as perfectly just and benevolent maker and ruler of such a world as this, can say little against Christianity but what can, with at least equal force, be retorted against themselves. Finding, therefore, no halting place in Deism, he remained in a state of perplexity, until, doubtless after many struggles, he yielded to the conviction, that, concerning the origin of things nothing whatever can be known. This is the only correct statement of his opinion; for dogmatic atheism he looked upon as absurd; as most of those, whom the world has considered Atheists, have always done. These particulars are important, because they show that my father's rejection of all that is called religious belief, was not, as many might suppose, primarily a matter of logic and evidence: the grounds of it were moral, still more than intellectual. He found it impossible to believe that a world so full of evil was the work of an Author combining infinite power with perfect goodness and righteousness. His intellect spurned the subtleties by which men attempt to blind themselves to this open contradiction. The Sabæan, or Manichæan theory of a Good and an Evil Principle, struggling against each other for the government of the universe, he would not have equally condemned; and I have heard him express surprise, that no one revived it in our time. He would have regarded it as a mere hypothesis; but he would have ascribed to it no depraving influence. As it was, his aversion to religion, in the sense usually attached to the term, was of the same kind with that of Lucretius: he regarded it with the feelings due not to a mere mental delusion, but to a great moral evil. He looked upon it as the greatest enemy of morality: first, by setting up fictitious excellences,—belief in creeds, devotional feelings, and ceremonies, not connected with the good of human-kind,—

and causing these to be accepted as substitutes for genuine virtues: but above all, by radically vitiating the standard of morals; making it consist in doing the will of a being, on whom it lavishes indeed all the phrases of adulation, but whom in sober truth it depicts as eminently hateful. I have a hundred times heard him say, that all ages and nations have represented their gods as wicked, in a constantly increasing progression, that mankind have gone on adding trait after trait till they reached the most perfect conception of wickedness which the human mind can devise, and have called this God, and prostrated themselves before it. This *ne plus ultra* of wickedness he considered to be embodied in what is commonly presented to mankind as the creed of Christianity. Think (he used to say) of a being who would make a Hell—who would create the human race with the infallible foreknowledge, and therefore with the intention, that the great majority of them were to be consigned to horrible and everlasting torment. The time, I believe, is drawing near when this dreadful conception of an object of worship will be no longer identified with Christianity; and when all persons, with any sense of moral good and evil, will look upon it with the same indignation with which my father regarded it. My father was as well aware as any one that Christians do not, in general, undergo the demoralizing consequences which seem inherent in such a creed, in the manner or to the extent which might have been expected from it. The same slovenliness of thought, and subjection of the reason to fears, wishes, and affections, which enable them to accept a theory involving a contradiction in terms, prevents them from perceiving the logical consequences of the theory. Such is the facility with which mankind believe at one and the same time things inconsistent with one another, and so few are those who draw from what they receive as truths, any consequences but those recommended to them by their feelings, that multitudes have held the undoubting belief in an Omnipotent Author of Hell, and have nevertheless identified that being with the best conception they were able to form of perfect goodness. Their worship was not paid to the demon which such a Being as they imagined would really be, but to their own ideal of excellence. The evil is, that such a belief keeps the ideal wretchedly low; and opposes the most obstinate resistance to all thought which has a tendency to raise it higher. Believers shrink from every train of ideas which would lead the mind to a clear conception and an elevated standard of excellence, because they feel (even when they do not distinctly see) that such a standard would conflict with many of the dispensations of nature, and with much of what they are accustomed to consider as the Christian creed. And thus morality continues a matter of blind tradition, with no consistent principle, nor even any consistent feeling, to guide it.

It would have been wholly inconsistent with my father's ideas of duty, to allow me to acquire impressions contrary to his convictions and feelings respecting religion: and he impressed upon me from the first, that the manner in which the world came into existence was a subject on which nothing was known: that the question, "Who made me?" cannot be answered, because we have no experience or authentic information from which to answer it; and that any answer only throws the difficulty a step further back, since the question immediately presents itself, "Who made God?" He, at the same time, took care that I should be acquainted with what had been thought by mankind on these impenetrable problems. I have mentioned at how early an age he made me a reader of ecclesiastical history; and he taught me to take the strongest interest in the

Reformation, as the great and decisive contest against priestly tyranny for liberty of thought.

I am thus one of the very few examples, in this country, of one who has not thrown off religious belief, but never had it: I grew up in a negative state with regard to it. I looked upon the modern exactly as I did upon the ancient religion, as something which in no way concerned me. It did not seem to me more strange that English people should believe what I did not, than that the men I read of in Herodotus should have done so. History had made the variety of opinions among mankind a fact familiar to me, and this was but a prolongation of that fact. This point in my early education had, however, incidentally one bad consequence deserving notice. In giving me an opinion contrary to that of the world, my father thought it necessary to give it as one which could not prudently be avowed to the world. This lesson of keeping my thoughts to myself, at that early age, was attended with some moral disadvantages; though my limited intercourse with strangers, especially such as were likely to speak to me on religion, prevented me from being placed in the alternative of avowal or hypocrisy. I remember two occasions in my boyhood, on which I felt myself in this alternative, and in both cases I avowed my disbelief and defended it. My opponents were boys, considerably older than myself: one of them I certainly staggered at the time, but the subject was never renewed between us: the other who was surprised and somewhat shocked, did his best to convince me for some time, without effect.

The great advance in liberty of discussion, which is one of the most important differences between the present time and that of my childhood, has greatly altered the moralities of this question; and I think that few men of my father's intellect and public spirit, holding with such intensity of moral conviction as he did, unpopular opinions on religion, or on any other of the great subjects of thought, would now either practise or inculcate the withholding of them from the world, unless in the cases, becoming fewer every day, in which frankness on these subjects would either risk the loss of means of subsistence, or would amount to exclusion from some sphere of usefulness peculiarly suitable to the capacities of the individual. On religion in particular the time appears to me to have come when it is the duty of all who, being qualified in point of knowledge, have on mature consideration satisfied themselves that the current opinions are not only false but hurtful, to make their dissent known; at least, if they are among those whose station or reputation gives their opinion a chance of being attended to. Such an avowal would put an end, at once and for ever, to the vulgar prejudice, that what is called, very improperly, unbelief, is connected with any bad qualities either of mind or heart. The world would be astonished if it knew how great a proportion of its brightest ornaments—of those most distinguished even in popular estimation for wisdom and virtue—are complete sceptics in religion; many of them refraining from avowal, less from personal considerations, than from a conscientious, though now in my opinion a most mistaken apprehension, lest by speaking out what would tend to weaken existing beliefs, and by consequence (as they suppose) existing restraints, they should do harm instead of good.

Of unbelievers (so called) as well as of believers, there are many species, including almost every variety of moral type. But the best among them, as no one who has had opportunities of really knowing them will hesitate to affirm, are more genuinely religious, in the best sense of the word religion, than those who exclusively arrogate to themselves the title. The liberality of the age, or in other words the weakening of the obstinate prejudice which makes men unable to see what is before their eyes because it is contrary to their expectations, has caused it to be very commonly admitted that a Deist may be truly religious: but if religion stands for any graces of character and not for mere dogma, the assertion may equally be made of many whose belief is far short of Deism. Though they may think the proof incomplete that the universe is a work of design, and though they assuredly disbelieve that it can have an Author and Governor who is *absolute* in power as well as perfect in goodness, they have that which constitutes the principal worth of all religions whatever, an ideal conception of a Perfect Being, to which they habitually refer as the guide of their conscience; and this ideal of Good is usually far nearer to perfection than the objective Deity of those, who think themselves obliged to find absolute goodness in the author of a world so crowded with suffering and so deformed by injustice as ours.

My father's moral convictions, wholly dissevered from religion, were very much of the character of those of the Greek philosophers; and were delivered with the force and decision which characterized all that came from him. Even at the very early age at which I read with him the *Memorabilia* of Xenophon, I imbibed from that work and from his comments a deep respect for the character of Socrates; who stood in my mind as a model of ideal excellence: and I well remember how my father at that time impressed upon me the lesson of the "Choice of Hercules." At a somewhat later period the lofty moral standard exhibited in the writings of Plato operated upon me with great force. My father's moral inculcations were at all times mainly those of the "Socratici viri"; justice, temperance (to which he gave a very extended application), veracity, perseverance, readiness to encounter pain and especially labour; regard for the public good; estimation of persons according to their merits, and of things according to their intrinsic usefulness; a life of exertion in contradiction to one of self-indulgent ease and sloth. These and other moralities he conveyed in brief sentences, uttered as occasion arose, of grave exhortation, or stern reprobation and contempt.

But though direct moral teaching does much, indirect does more; and the effect my father produced on my character, did not depend solely on what he said or did with that direct object, but also, and still more, on what manner of man he was.

In his views of life he partook of the character of the Stoic, the Epicurean, and the Cynic, not in the modern but the ancient sense of the word. In his personal qualities the Stoic predominated. His standard of morals was Epicurean, inasmuch as it was utilitarian, taking as the exclusive test of right and wrong, the tendency of actions to produce pleasure or pain. But he had (and this was the Cynic element) scarcely any belief in pleasure; at least in his later years, of which alone, on this point, I can speak confidently. He was not insensible to pleasures; but he deemed very few of them worth the price which, at least in the present state of society, must be paid for them. The greater number of miscarriages in life, he considered to be attributable to the over-valuing of pleasures. Accordingly, temperance, in the large sense intended by the Greek philosophers—stopping short at the point of moderation in all indulgences—was with him, as with them, almost the central point of educational precept. His inculcations of this virtue fill a large place in my childish remembrances. He thought human life a poor thing at best, after the freshness of youth and of unsatisfied curiosity had gone by. This was a topic on which he did not often speak, especially, it may be supposed, in the presence of young persons: but when he did, it was with an air of settled and profound conviction. He would sometimes say, that if life were made what it might be, by good government and good education, it would be worth having: but he never spoke with anything like enthusiasm even of that possibility. He never varied in rating intellectual enjoyments above all others, even in value as pleasures, independently of their ulterior benefits. The pleasures of the benevolent affections he placed high in the scale; and used to say, that he had never known a happy old man, except those who were able to live over again in the pleasures of the young. For passionate emotions of all sorts, and for everything which has been said or written in exaltation of them, he professed the greatest contempt. He regarded them as a form of madness. "The intense" was with him a bye-word of scornful disapprobation. He regarded as an aberration of the moral standard of modern times, compared with that of the ancients, the great stress laid upon feeling. Feelings, as such, he considered to be no proper subjects of praise or blame. Right and wrong, good and bad, he regarded as qualities solely of conduct—of acts and omissions; there being no feeling which may not lead, and does not frequently lead, either to good or to bad actions: conscience itself, the very desire to act right, often leading people to act wrong. Consistently carrying out the doctrine, that the object of praise and blame should be the discouragement of wrong conduct and the encouragement of right, he refused to let his praise or blame be influenced by the motive of the agent. He blamed as severely what he thought a bad action, when the motive was a feeling of duty, as if the agents had been consciously evil doers. He would not have accepted as a plea in mitigation for inquisitors, that they sincerely believed burning heretics to be an obligation of conscience. But though he did not allow honesty of purpose to soften his disapprobation of actions, it had its full effect on his estimation of characters. No one prized conscientiousness and rectitude of intention more highly, or was more incapable of valuing any person in whom he did not feel assurance of it. But he disliked people quite as much for any other deficiency, provided he thought it equally likely to make them act ill. He disliked, for instance, a fanatic in any bad cause, as much or more than one who adopted the same cause from self-interest, because he thought him even more likely to be practically mischievous. And thus, his aversion to many intellectual errors, or what he regarded as such, partook, in a certain sense, of the character of a moral feeling. All this is merely saying that he, in a degree once common, but now very unusual, threw his feelings into his opinions; which truly it is difficult to understand how any one who possesses much of both, can fail to do. None but those who do not care about opinions, will confound this with intolerance. Those, who having opinions which they hold to be immensely important, and their contraries to be prodigiously hurtful, have any deep regard for the general good, will necessarily dislike as a class and in the abstract, those who think wrong what they think right, and right what they think wrong: though they need not therefore be, nor was my father, insensible to good qualities in an opponent, nor governed in their estimation of individuals by one general presumption, instead of by the whole of their character. I grant that an earnest person, being no more infallible than other men, is liable to dislike people on account of opinions which do not merit dislike; but if he neither himself does them any ill office, nor connives at its being done by others, he is not intolerant: and the forbearance which flows from a conscientious sense of the importance to mankind of the equal freedom of all opinions, is the only tolerance which is commendable, or, to the highest moral order of minds, possible.

It will be admitted, that a man of the opinions, and the character, above described, was likely to leave a strong moral impression on any mind principally formed by him, and that his moral teaching was not likely to err on the side of laxity or indulgence. The element which was chiefly deficient in his moral relation to his children was that of tenderness. I do not believe that this deficiency lay in his own nature. I believe him to have had much more feeling than he habitually showed, and much greater capacities of feeling than were ever developed. He resembled most Englishmen in being ashamed of the signs of feeling, and by the absence of demonstration, starving the feelings themselves. If we consider further that he was in the trying position of sole teacher, and add to this that his temper was constitutionally irritable, it is impossible not to feel true pity for a father who did, and strove to do, so much for his children, who would have so valued their affection, yet who must have been constantly feeling that fear of him was drying it up at its source. This was no longer the case later in life, and with his younger children. They loved him tenderly: and if I cannot say so much of myself, I was always loyally devoted to him. As regards my own education, I hesitate to pronounce whether I was more a loser or gainer by his severity. It was not such as to prevent me from having a happy childhood. And I do not believe that boys can be induced to apply themselves with vigour, and what is so much more difficult, perseverance, to dry and irksome studies, by the sole force of persuasion and soft words. Much must be done, and much must be learnt, by children, for which rigid discipline, and known liability to punishment, are indispensable as means. It is, no doubt, a very laudable effort, in modern teaching, to render as much as possible of what the young are required to learn, easy and interesting to them. But when this principle is pushed to the length of not requiring them to learn anything *but* what has been made easy and interesting, one of the chief objects of education is sacrificed. I rejoice in the decline of the old brutal and tyrannical system of teaching, which, however, did succeed in enforcing habits of application; but the new, as it seems to me, is training up a race of men who will be incapable of doing anything which is disagreeable to them. I do not, then, believe that fear, as an element in education, can be dispensed with; but I am sure that it ought not to be the main element; and when it predominates so much as to preclude love and confidence on the part of the child to those who should be the unreservedly trusted advisers of after years, and perhaps to seal up the fountains of frank and spontaneous communicativeness in the child's nature, it is an evil for which a large abatement must be made from the benefits, moral and intellectual, which may flow from any other part of the education.

During this first period of my life, the habitual frequenters of my father's house were limited to a very few persons, most of them little known to the world, but whom personal worth, and more or less of congeniality with at least his political opinions (not so frequently to be met with then as since) inclined him to cultivate; and his conversations with them I listened to with interest and instruction. My being an habitual inmate of my father's study made me acquainted with the dearest of his friends, David Ricardo, who by his benevolent countenance, and kindliness of manner, was very attractive to young persons, and who, after I became a student of political economy, invited me to his house and to walk with him in order to converse on the subject. I was a more frequent visitor (from about 1817 or 1818) to Mr. Hume, who, born in the same part of Scotland as my father, and having been, I rather think, a younger schoolfellow or college companion of his, had on returning from India renewed their youthful acquaintance, and who, coming like many others greatly under the influence of my father's intellect and energy of character, was induced partly by that influence to go into Parliament, and there adopt the line of conduct which has given him an honourable place in the history of his country. Of Mr. Bentham I saw much more, owing to the close intimacy which existed between him and my father. I do not know how soon after my father's first arrival in England they became acquainted. But my father was the earliest Englishman of any great mark, who thoroughly understood, and in the main adopted, Bentham's general views of ethics, government and law: and this was a natural foundation for sympathy between them, and made them familiar companions in a period of Bentham's life during which he admitted much fewer visitors than was the case subsequently. At this time Mr. Bentham passed some part of every year at Barrow Green House, in a beautiful part of the Surrey Hills, a few miles from Godstone, and there I each summer accompanied my father in a long visit. In 1813 Mr. Bentham, my father, and I made an excursion, which included Oxford, Bath and Bristol, Exeter, Plymouth, and Portsmouth. In this journey I saw many things which were instructive to me, and acquired my first taste for natural scenery, in the elementary form of fondness for a "view." In the succeeding winter we moved into a house very near Mr. Bentham's, which my father rented from him, in Queen Square, Westminster. From 1814 to 1817 Mr. Bentham lived during half of each year at Ford Abbey, in Somersetshire (or rather in a part of Devonshire surrounded by Somersetshire), which intervals I had the advantage of passing at that place. This sojourn was, I think, an important circumstance in my education. Nothing contributes more to nourish elevation of sentiments in a people, than the large and free character of their habitations. The middle-age architecture, the baronial hall, and the spacious and lofty rooms, of this fine old place, so unlike the mean and cramped externals of English middle class life, gave the sentiment of a larger and freer existence, and were to me a sort of poetic cultivation, aided also by the character of the grounds in which the Abbey stood; which were *riant* and secluded, umbrageous, and full of the sound of falling waters.

I owed another of the fortunate circumstances in my education, a year's residence in France, to Mr. Bentham's brother, General Sir Samuel Bentham. I had seen Sir Samuel Bentham and his family at their house near Gosport in the course of the tour already mentioned (he being then Superintendent of the Dockyard at Portsmouth), and during a stay of a few days which they made at Ford Abbey shortly after the peace, before going to live on the Continent. In 1820 they invited me for a six months' visit to them in the South of France, which their kindness ultimately prolonged to nearly a twelvemonth. Sir Samuel Bentham, though of a character of mind different from that of his illustrious brother, was a man of very considerable attainments and general powers, with a decided genius for mechanical art. His wife, a daughter of the celebrated chemist, Dr. Fordyce, was a woman of strong will and decided character, much general knowledge, and great practical good sense of the Edgeworth kind: she was the ruling spirit of the household, as she deserved, and was well qualified, to be. Their family consisted of one son (the eminent botanist) and three daughters, the youngest about two years my senior. I am indebted to them for much and various instruction, and for an almost parental interest in my welfare. When I first joined them, in May 1820, they occupied the Château of Pompignan (still belonging to a descendant of Voltaire's enemy) on the heights overlooking the plain of the Garonne between Montauban and Toulouse. I accompanied them in an excursion to the Pyrenees, including a stay of some duration at Bagnères de Bigorre, a journey to Pau, Bayonne, and Bagnères de Luchon, and an ascent of the Pic du Midi de Bigorre.

This first introduction to the highest order of mountain scenery made the deepest impression on me, and gave a colour to my tastes through life. In October we proceeded by the beautiful mountain route of Castres and St. Pons, from Toulouse to Montpellier, in which last neighbour-hood Sir Samuel had just bought the estate of Restinclière, near the foot of the singular mountain of St. Loup. During this residence in France I acquired a familiar knowledge of the French language, and acquaintance with the ordinary French literature; I took lessons in various bodily exercises, in none of which however I made any proficiency; and at Montpellier I attended the excellent winter courses of lectures at the Faculté des Sciences, those of M. Anglada on chemistry, of M. Provençal on zoology, and of a very accomplished representative of the eighteenth century meta-physics, M. Gergonne, on logic, under the name of Philo-sophy of the Sciences. I also went through a course of the higher mathematics under the private tuition of M. Len-théric, a professor at the Lycée of Montpellier. But the greatest, perhaps, of the many advantages which I owed to this episode in my education, was that of having breathed for a whole year, the free and genial atmosphere of Conti-nental life. This advantage was not the less real though I could not then estimate, nor even consciously feel it. Having so little experience of English life, and the few people I

knew being mostly such as had public objects, of a large
and personally disinterested kind, at heart, I was ignorant
of the low moral tone of what, in England, is called society;
the habit of, not indeed professing, but taking for granted
in every mode of implication, that conduct is of course
always directed towards low and petty objects; the absence
of high feelings which manifests itself by sneering depre-
ciation of all demonstrations of them, and by general
abstinence (except among a few of the stricter religionists)
from professing any high principles of action at all, except
in those preordained cases in which such profession is put
on as part of the costume and formalities of the occasion.
I could not then know or estimate the difference between
this manner of existence, and that of a people like the
French, whose faults, if equally real, are at all events
different; among whom sentiments, which by comparison
at least may be called elevated, are the current coin of
human intercourse, both in books and in private life; and
though often evaporating in profession, are yet kept alive
in the nation at large by constant exercise, and stimulated
by sympathy, so as to form a living and active part of the
existence of great numbers of persons, and to be recognised
and understood by all. Neither could I then appreciate the
general culture of the understanding, which results from
the habitual exercise of the feelings, and is thus carried
down into the most uneducated classes of several countries
on the Continent, in a degree not equalled in England
among the so-called educated, except where an unusual
tenderness of conscience leads to a habitual exercise of the
intellect on questions of right and wrong. I did not know
the way in which, among the ordinary English, the absence
of interest in things of an unselfish kind, except occasionally
in a special thing here and there, and the habit of not
speaking to others, nor much even to themselves, about the

things in which they do feel interest, causes both their feelings and their intellectual faculties to remain undeveloped, or to develope themselves only in some single and very limited direction; reducing them, considered as spiritual beings, to a kind of negative existence. All these things I did not perceive till long afterwards; but I even then felt, though without stating it clearly to myself, the contrast between the frank sociability and amiability of French personal intercourse, and the English mode of existence in which everybody acts as if everybody else (with few, or no exceptions) was either an enemy or a bore. In France, it is true, the bad as well as the good points, both of individual and of national character, come more to the surface, and break out more fearlessly in ordinary intercourse, than in England: but the general habit of the people is to show, as well as to expect, friendly feeling in every one towards every other, wherever there is not some positive cause for the opposite. In England it is only of the best bred people, in the upper or upper middle ranks, that anything like this can be said.

In my way through Paris, both going and returning, I passed some time in the house of M. Say, the eminent political economist, who was a friend and correspondent of my father, having become acquainted with him on a visit to England a year or two after the peace. He was a man of the later period of the French Revolution, a fine specimen of the best kind of French Republican, one of those who had never bent the knee to Bonaparte though courted by him to do so; a truly upright, brave, and enlightened man. He lived a quiet and studious life, made happy by warm affections, public and private. He was acquainted with many of the chiefs of the Liberal party, and I saw various noteworthy persons while staying at his house; among whom I have pleasure in the recollection of having once seen Saint-Simon, not yet the founder either of a philosophy or a religion, and considered only as a clever *original*. The chief fruit which I carried away from the society I saw, was a strong and permanent interest in Continental Liberalism, of which I ever afterwards kept myself *au courant*, as much as of English politics: a thing not at all usual in those days with Englishmen, and which had a very salutary influence on my development, keeping me free from the error always prevalent in England, and from which even my father with all his superiority to prejudice was not exempt, of judging universal questions by a merely English standard. After passing a few weeks at Caen with an old friend of my father's, I returned to England in July 1821; and my education resumed its ordinary course.

III

A CRISIS IN MY MENTAL HISTORY.
ONE STAGE ONWARD

For some years after this time I wrote very little, and nothing regularly, for publication: and great were the advantages which I derived from the intermission. It was of no common importance to me, at this period, to be able to digest and mature my thoughts for my own mind only, without any immediate call for giving them out in print. Had I gone on writing, it would have much disturbed the important transformation in my opinions and character, which took place during those years. The origin of this transformation, or at least the process by which I was prepared for it, can only be explained by turning some distance back.

From the winter of 1821, when I first read Bentham, and especially from the commencement of the *Westminster*

Review, I had what might truly be called an object in life; to be a reformer of the world. My conception of my own happiness was entirely identified with this object. The personal sympathies I wished for were those of fellow labourers in this enterprise. I endeavoured to pick up as many flowers as I could by the way; but as a serious and permanent personal satisfaction to rest upon, my whole reliance was placed on this; and I was accustomed to felicitate myself on the certainty of a happy life which I enjoyed, through placing my happiness in something durable and distant, in which some progress might be always making, while it could never be exhausted by complete attainment. This did very well for several years, during which the general improvement going on in the world and the idea of myself as engaged with others in struggling to promote it, seemed enough to fill up an interesting and animated existence. But the time came when I awakened from this as from a dream. It was in the autumn of 1826. I was in a dull state of nerves, such as everybody is occasionally liable to; unsusceptible to enjoyment or pleasurable excitement; one of those moods when what is pleasure at other times, becomes insipid or indifferent; the state, I should think, in which converts to Methodism usually are, when smitten by their first "conviction of sin." In this frame of mind it occurred to me to put the question directly to myself: "Suppose that all your objects in life were realized; that all the changes in institutions and opinions which you are looking forward to, could be completely effected at this very instant: would this be a great joy and happiness to you?" And an irrepressible self-consciousness distinctly answered, "No!" At this my heart sank within me: the whole foundation on which my life was constructed fell down. All my happiness was to have been found in the continual pursuit of this end. The end had ceased to charm, and how could there ever again be any interest in the means? I seemed to have nothing left to live for.

At first I hoped that the cloud would pass away of itself; but it did not. A night's sleep, the sovereign remedy for the smaller vexations of life, had no effect on it. I awoke to a renewed consciousness of the woful fact. I carried it with me into all companies, into all occupations. Hardly anything had power to cause me even a few minutes' oblivion of it. For some months the cloud seemed to grow thicker and thicker. The lines in Coleridge's *Dejection*— I was not then acquainted with them—exactly describe my case:

> A grief without a pang, void, dark and drear,
> A drowsy, stifled, unimpassioned grief,
> Which finds no natural outlet or relief
> In word, or sigh, or tear.

In vain I sought relief from my favourite books; those memorials of past nobleness and greatness from which I had always hitherto drawn strength and animation. I read them now without feeling, or with the accustomed feeling *minus* all its charm; and I became persuaded, that my love of mankind, and of excellence for its own sake, had worn itself out. I sought no comfort by speaking to others of what I felt. If I had loved any one sufficiently to make confiding my griefs a necessity, I should not have been in the condition I was. I felt, too, that mine was not an interesting, or in any way respectable distress. There was nothing in it to attract sympathy. Advice, if I had known where to seek it, would have been most precious. The words of Macbeth to the physician often occurred to my thoughts. But there was no one on whom I could build the faintest hope of such assistance. My father, to whom it would have been natural to me to have recourse in any practical diffi- culties, was the last person to whom, in such a case as this,

I looked for help. Everything convinced me that he had no knowledge of any such mental state as I was suffering from, and that even if he could be made to understand it, he was not the physician who could heal it. My education, which was wholly his work, had been conducted without any regard to the possibility of its ending in this result; and I saw no use in giving him the pain of thinking that his plans had failed, when the failure was probably irremediable, and, at all events, beyond the power of *his* remedies. Of other friends, I had at that time none to whom I had any hope of making my condition intelligible. It was however abundantly intelligible to myself; and the more I dwelt upon it, the more hopeless it appeared.

My course of study had led me to believe, that all mental and moral feelings and qualities, whether of a good or of a bad kind, were the results of association; that we love one thing, and hate another, take pleasure in one sort of action or contemplation, and pain in another sort, through the clinging of pleasurable or painful ideas to those things, from the effect of education or of experience. As a corollary from this, I had always heard it maintained by my father, and was myself convinced, that the object of education should be to form the strongest possible associations of the salutary class; associations of pleasure with all things beneficial to the great whole, and of pain with all things hurtful to it. This doctrine appeared inexpugnable; but it now seemed to me, on retrospect, that my teachers had occupied themselves but superficially with the means of forming and keeping up these salutary associations. They seemed to have trusted altogether to the old familiar instruments, praise and blame, reward and punishment. Now, I did not doubt that by these means, begun early, and applied unremittingly, intense associations of pain and pleasure, especially of pain, might be created, and might produce desires and aversions capable of lasting undiminished to the end of life. But there must always be something artificial and casual in associations thus produced. The pains and pleasures thus forcibly associated with things, are not connected with them by any natural tie; and it is therefore, I thought, essential to the durability of these associations, that they should have become so intense and inveterate as to be practically indissoluble, before the habitual exercise of the power of analysis had commenced. For I now saw, or thought I saw, what I had always before received with incredulity—that the habit of analysis has a tendency to wear away the feelings: as indeed it has, when no other mental habit is cultivated, and the analysing spirit remains without its natural complements and correctives. The very excellence of analysis (I argued) is that it tends to weaken and undermine whatever is the result of prejudice; that it enables us mentally to separate ideas which have only casually clung together: and no associations whatever could ultimately resist this dissolving force, were it not that we owe to analysis our clearest knowledge of the permanent sequences in nature; the real connexions between Things, not dependent on our will and feelings; natural laws, by virtue of which, in many cases, one thing is inseparable from another in fact; which laws, in proportion as they are clearly perceived and imaginatively realized, cause our ideas of things which are always joined together in Nature, to cohere more and more closely in our thoughts. Analytic habits may thus even strengthen the associations between causes and effects, means and ends, but tend altogether to weaken those which are, to speak familiarly, a *mere* matter of feeling. They are therefore (I thought) favourable to prudence and clear-sightedness, but a perpetual worm at the root both of the passions and of the virtues; and, above all, fearfully undermine all desires, and all pleasures, which

are the effects of association, that is, according to the theory
I held, all except the purely physical and organic; of the
entire insufficiency of which to make life desirable, no one
had a stronger conviction than I had. These were the laws
of human nature, by which, as it seemed to me, I had been
brought to my present state. All those to whom I looked
up, were of opinion that the pleasure of sympathy with
human beings, and the feelings which made the good of
others, and especially of mankind on a large scale, the object
of existence, were the greatest and surest sources of happiness. Of the truth of this I was convinced, but to know
that a feeling would make me happy if I had it, did not give
me the feeling. My education, I thought, had failed to
create these feelings in sufficient strength to resist the dissolving influence of analysis, while the whole course of my
intellectual cultivation had made precocious and premature
analysis the inveterate habit of my mind. I was thus, as I
said to myself, left stranded at the commencement of my
voyage, with a well-equipped ship and a rudder, but no sail;
without any real desire for the ends which I had been so
carefully fitted out to work for: no delight in virtue, or the
general good, but also just as little in anything else. The
fountains of vanity and ambition seemed to have dried up
within me, as completely as those of benevolence. I had
had (as I reflected) some gratification of vanity at too early
an age: I had obtained some distinction, and felt myself of
some importance, before the desire of distinction and of
importance had grown into a passion: and little as it was
which I had attained, yet having been attained too early,
like all pleasures enjoyed too soon, it had made me *blasé*
and indifferent to the pursuit. Thus neither selfish nor unselfish pleasures were pleasures to me. And there seemed
no power in nature sufficient to begin the formation of my
character anew, and create in a mind now irretrievably

analytic, fresh associations of pleasure with any of the objects of human desire.

These were the thoughts which mingled with the dry heavy dejection of the melancholy winter of 1826–7. During this time I was not incapable of my usual occupations. I went on with them mechanically, by the mere force of habit. I had been so drilled in a certain sort of mental exercise, that I could still carry it on when all the spirit had gone out of it. I even composed and spoke several speeches at the debating society, how, or with what degree of success, I know not. Of four years continual speaking at that society, this is the only year of which I remember next to nothing. Two lines of Coleridge, in whom alone of all writers I have found a true description of what I felt, were often in my thoughts, not at this time (for I had never read them), but in a later period of the same mental malady:

> Work without hope draws nectar in a sieve,
> And hope without an object cannot live.

In all probability my case was by no means so peculiar as I fancied it, and I doubt not that many others have passed through a similar state; but the idiosyncrasies of my education had given to the general phenomenon a special character, which made it seem the natural effect of causes that it was hardly possible for time to remove. I frequently asked myself, if I could, or if I was bound to go on living, when life must be passed in this manner. I generally answered to myself, that I did not think I could possibly bear it beyond a year. When, however, not more than half that duration of time had elapsed, a small ray of light broke in upon my gloom. I was reading, accidentally, Marmontel's *Mémoires*, and came to the passage which relates his father's death, the distressed position of the

-family, and the sudden inspiration by which he, then a mere boy, felt and made them feel that he would be everything to them—would supply the place of all that they had lost. A vivid conception of the scene and its feelings came over me, and I was moved to tears. From this moment my burden grew lighter. The oppression of the thought that all feeling was dead within me, was gone. I was no longer hopeless: I was not a stock or a stone. I had still, it seemed, some of the material out of which all worth of character, and all capacity for happiness, are made. Relieved from my ever present sense of irremediable wretchedness, I gradually found that the ordinary incidents of life could again give me some pleasure; that I could again find enjoyment, not intense, but sufficient for cheerfulness, in sunshine and sky, in books, in conversation, in public affairs; and that there was, once more, excitement, though of a moderate kind, in exerting myself for my opinions, and for the public good. Thus the cloud gradually drew off, and I again enjoyed life: and though I had several relapses, some of which lasted many months, I never again was as miserable as I had been.

The experiences of this period had two very marked effects on my opinions and character. In the first place, they led me to adopt a theory of life, very unlike that on which I had before acted, and having much in common with what at that time I certainly had never heard of, the anti-self-consciousness theory of Carlyle. I never, indeed, wavered in the conviction that happiness is the test of all rules of conduct, and the end of life. But I now thought that this end was only to be attained by not making it the direct end. Those only are happy (I thought) who have their minds fixed on some object other than their own happiness; on the happiness of others, on the improvement of mankind, even on some art or pursuit, followed not as a means, but as itself an ideal end. Aiming thus at something else, they find happiness by the way. The enjoyments of life (such was now my theory) are sufficient to make it a pleasant thing, when they are taken *en passant*, without being made a principal object. Once make them so, and they are immediately felt to be insufficient. They will not bear a scrutinizing examination. Ask yourself whether you are happy, and you cease to be so. The only chance is to treat, not happiness, but some end external to it, as the purpose of life. Let your self-consciousness, your scrutiny, your self-interrogation, exhaust themselves on that; and if otherwise fortunately circumstanced you will inhale happiness with the air you breathe, without dwelling on it or thinking about it, without either forestalling it in imagination, or putting it to flight by fatal questioning. This theory now became the basis of my philosophy of life. And I still hold to it as the best theory for all those who have but a moderate degree of sensibility and of capacity for enjoyment, that is, for the great majority of mankind.

The other important change which my opinions at this time underwent, was that I, for the first time, gave its proper place, among the prime necessities of human well-being, to the internal culture of the individual. I ceased to attach almost exclusive importance to the ordering of outward circumstances, and the training of the human being for speculation and for action.

I had now learnt by experience that the passive susceptibilities needed to be cultivated as well as the active capacities, and required to be nourished and enriched as well as guided. I did not, for an instant, lose sight of, or undervalue, that part of the truth which I had seen before; I never turned recreant to intellectual culture, or ceased to consider the power and practice of analysis as an essential condition both of individual and of social improvement.

But I thought that it had consequences which required to be corrected, by joining other kinds of cultivation with it. The maintenance of a due balance among the faculties now seemed to me of primary importance. The cultivation of the feelings became one of the cardinal points in my ethical and philosophical creed. And my thoughts and inclinations turned in an increasing degree towards whatever seemed capable of being instrumental to that object.

I now began to find meaning in the things which I had read or heard about the importance of poetry and art as instruments of human culture. But it was some time longer before I began to know this by personal experience. The only one of the imaginative arts in which I had from childhood taken great pleasure, was music; the best effect of which (and in this it surpasses perhaps every other art) consists in exciting enthusiasm; in winding up to a high pitch those feelings of an elevated kind which are already in the character, but to which this excitement gives a glow and a fervour, which, though transitory at its utmost height, is precious for sustaining them at other times. This effect of music I had often experienced; but like all my pleasurable susceptibilities it was suspended during the gloomy period. I had sought relief again and again from this quarter, but found none. After the tide had turned, and I was in process of recovery, I had been helped forward by music, but in a much less elevated manner. I at this time first became acquainted with Weber's *Oberon*, and the extreme pleasure which I drew from its delicious melodies did me good, by showing me a source of pleasure to which I was as susceptible as ever. The good, however, was much impaired by the thought that the pleasure of music (as is quite true of such pleasure as this was, that of mere tune) fades with familiarity, and requires either to be revived by intermittence, or fed by continual novelty. And it is very characteristic both of my then state, and of the general tone of my mind at this period of my life, that I was seriously tormented by the thought of the exhaustibility of musical combinations. The octave consists only of five tones and two semitones, which can be put together in only a limited number of ways, of which but a small proportion are beautiful: most of these, it seemed to me, must have been already discovered, and there could not be room for a long succession of Mozarts and Webers, to strike out, as these had done, entirely new and surpassingly rich veins of musical beauty. This source of anxiety may, perhaps, be thought to resemble that of the philosophers of Laputa, who feared lest the sun should be burnt out. It was, however, connected with the best feature in my character, and the only good point to be found in my very unromantic and in no way honourable distress. For though my dejection, honestly looked at, could not be called other than egotistical, produced by the ruin, as I thought, of my fabric of happiness, yet the destiny of mankind in general was ever in my thoughts, and could not be separated from my own. I felt that the flaw in my life, must be a flaw in life itself; that the question was, whether, if the reformers of society and government could succeed in their objects, and every person in the community were free and in a state of physical comfort, the pleasures of life, being no longer kept up by struggle and privation, would cease to be pleasures. And I felt that unless I could see my way to some better hope than this for human happiness in general, my dejection must continue; but that if I could see such an outlet, I should then look on the world with pleasure; content as far as I was myself concerned, with any fair share of the general lot.

This state of my thoughts and feelings made the fact of

my reading Wordsworth for the first time (in the autumn of 1828), an important event in my life. I took up the collection of his poems from curiosity, with no expectation of mental relief from it, though I had before resorted to poetry with that hope. In the worst period of my depression, I had read through the whole of Byron (then new to me), to try whether a poet, whose peculiar department was supposed to be that of the intenser feelings, could rouse any feeling in me. As might be expected, I got no good from this reading, but the reverse. The poet's state of mind was too like my own. His was the lament of a man who had worn out all pleasures, and who seemed to think that life, to all who possess the good things of it, must necessarily be the vapid, uninteresting thing which I found it. His Harold and Manfred had the same burden on them which I had; and I was not in a frame of mind to desire any comfort from the vehement sensual passion of his Giaours, or the sullenness of his Laras. But while Byron was exactly what did not suit my condition, Wordsworth was exactly what did. I had looked into the *Excursion* two or three years before, and found little in it; and I should probably have found as little, had I read it at this time. But the miscellaneous poems, in the two-volume edition of 1815 (to which little of value was added in the latter part of the author's life), proved to be the precise thing for my mental wants at that particular juncture.

In the first place, these poems addressed themselves powerfully to one of the strongest of my pleasurable susceptibilities, the love of rural objects and natural scenery; to which I had been indebted not only for much of the pleasure of my life, but quite recently for relief from one of my longest relapses into depression. In this power of rural beauty over me, there was a foundation laid for taking pleasure in Wordsworth's poetry; the more so, as his scenery lies mostly among mountains, which, owing to my early Pyrenean excursion, were my ideal of natural beauty. But Wordsworth would never have had any great effect on me, if he had merely placed before me beautiful pictures of natural scenery. Scott does this still better than Wordsworth, and a very second-rate landscape does it more effectually than any poet. What made Wordsworth's poems a medicine for my state of mind, was that they expressed, not mere outward beauty, but states of feeling, and of thought coloured by feeling, under the excitement of beauty. They seemed to be the very culture of the feelings, which I was in quest of. In them I seemed to draw from a source of inward joy, of sympathetic and imaginative pleasure, which could be shared in by all human beings; which had no connexion with struggle or imperfection, but would be made richer by every improvement in the physical or social condition of mankind. From them I seemed to learn what would be the perennial sources of happiness, when all the greater evils of life shall have been removed. And I felt myself at once better and happier as I came under their influence. There have certainly been, even in our own age, greater poets than Wordsworth; but poetry of deeper and loftier feeling could not have done for me at that time what his did. I needed to be made to feel that there was real, permanent happiness in tranquil contemplation. Wordsworth taught me this, not only without turning away from, but with a greatly increased interest in the common feelings and common destiny of human beings. And the delight which these poems gave me, proved that with culture of this sort, there was nothing to dread from the most confirmed habit of analysis. At the conclusion of the Poems came the famous Ode, falsely called Platonic, *Imtimations of Immortality*: in which, along with more than his usual sweetness of melody and rhythm, and along with the

two passages of grand imagery but bad philosophy so often
quoted, I found that he too had had similar experience to
mine; that he also had felt that the first freshness of youthful
enjoyment of life was not lasting; but that he had sought
for compensation, and found it, in the way in which he
was now teaching me to find it. The result was that I
gradually, but completely, emerged from my habitual depression, and was never again subject to it. I long continued to value Wordsworth less according to his intrinsic
merits, than by the measure of what he had done for me.
Compared with the greatest poets, he may be said to be
the poet of unpoetical natures, possessed of quiet and con-
templative tastes. But unpoetical natures are precisely
those which require poetic cultivation. This cultivation
Wordsworth is much more fitted to give, than poets who
are intrinsically far more poets than he.

J. S. MILL'S INAUGURAL ADDRESS AT ST ANDREWS

In complying with the custom which prescribes that the person whom you have called by your suffrages to the honorary presidency of your University should embody in an Address a few thoughts on the subjects which most nearly concern a seat of liberal education; let me begin by saying, that this usage appears to me highly commendable. Education, in its larger sense, is one of the most inexhaustible of all topics. Though there is hardly any subject on which so much has been written, by so many of the wisest men, it is as fresh to those who come to it with a fresh mind, a mind not hopelessly filled full with other people's conclusions, as it was to the first explorers of it: and notwithstanding the great mass of excellent things which have been said respecting it, no thoughtful person finds any lack of things both great and small still waiting to be said, or waiting to be developed and followed out to their consequences. Education, moreover, is one of the subjects which most essentially require to be considered by various minds, and from a variety of points of view. For, of all many-sided subjects, it is the one which has the greatest number of sides. Not only does it include whatever we do for ourselves, and whatever is done for us by others, for the express purpose of bringing us somewhat nearer to the perfection of our nature; it does more: in its largest acceptation, it comprehends even the indirect effects produced on character and on the human faculties, by things of which the direct purposes are quite different; by laws, by forms of government, by the industrial arts, by modes of social life; nay even by physical facts not dependent on human will; by climate, soil, and local position. Whatever helps to shape the human being; to make the individual what he is, or hinder him from being what he is not—is part of his education. And a very bad education it often is; requiring all that can be done by cultivated intelligence and will, to counteract its tendencies. To take an obvious instance; the niggardliness of Nature in some places, by engrossing the whole energies of the human being in the mere preservation of life, and her over-bounty in others, affording a sort of brutish subsistence on too easy terms, with hardly any exertion of the human faculties, are both hostile to the spontaneous growth and development of the mind; and it is at those two extremes of the scale that we find human societies in the state of most unmitigated savagery. I shall confine myself, however, to education in the narrower sense; the culture which each generation purposely gives to those who are to be its successors, in order to qualify them for at least keeping up, and if possible for raising, the level of improvement which has been attained. Nearly all here present are daily occupied either in receiving or in giving this sort of education: and the part of it which most concerns you at present is that in which you are yourselves engaged—the stage of education which is the appointed business of a national University.

The proper function of an University in national education is tolerably well understood. At least there is a tolerably general agreement about what an University is not. It is not a place of professional education. Universities are not intended to teach the knowledge required to fit men for some special mode of gaining their livelihood. Their object is not to make skilful lawyers, or physicians, or engineers, but capable and cultivated human beings. It is very right that there should be public facilities for the study of professions. It is well that there should be Schools of

Law, and of Medicine, and it would be well if there were schools of engineering, and the industrial arts. The countries which have such institutions are greatly the better for them; and there is something to be said for having them in the same localities, and under the same general super-intendence, as the establishments devoted to education properly so called. But these things are no part of what every generation owes to the next, as that on which its civilization and worth will principally depend. They are needed only by a comparatively few, who are under the strongest private inducements to acquire them by their own efforts; and even those few do not require them until after their education, in the ordinary sense, has been completed. Whether those whose speciality they are, will learn them as a branch of intelligence or as a mere trade, and whether, having learnt them, they will make a wise and conscien-tious use of them or the reverse, depends less on the manner in which they are taught their profession, than upon what sort of minds they bring to it—what kind of intelligence, and of conscience, the general system of education has developed in them. Men are men before they are lawyers, or physicians, or merchants, or manufacturers; and if you make them capable and sensible men, they will make them-selves capable and sensible lawyers or physicians. What professional men should carry away with them from an University, is not professional knowledge, but that which should direct the use of their professional knowledge, and bring the light of general culture to illuminate the techni-calities of a special pursuit. Men may be competent lawyers without general education, but it depends on general education to make them philosophic lawyers—who de-mand, and are capable of apprehending, principles, instead of merely cramming their memory with details. And so of all other useful pursuits, mechanical included. Education makes a man a more intelligent shoemaker, if that be his occupation, but not by teaching him how to make shoes; it does so by the mental exercise it gives, and the habits it impresses.

This, then, is what a mathematician would call the higher limit of University education: its province ends where education, ceasing to be general, branches off into departments adapted to the individual's destination in life. The lower limit is more difficult to define. An University is not concerned with elementary instruction: the pupil is supposed to have acquired that before coming here. But where does elementary instruction end, and the higher studies begin? Some have given a very wide extension to the idea of elementary instruction. According to them, it is not the office of an University to give instruction in single branches of knowledge from the commencement. What the pupil should be taught here (they think), is to methodize his knowledge: to look at every separate part of it in its relation to the other parts, and to the whole; combining the partial glimpses which he has obtained of the field of human knowledge at different points, into a general map, if I may so speak, of the entire region; observing how all knowledge is connected, how we ascend to one branch by means of another, how the higher modifies the lower, and the lower helps us to understand the higher; how every existing reality is a compound of many properties, of which each science or distinct mode of study reveals but a small part, but the whole of which must be included to enable us to know it truly as a fact in Nature, and not as a mere abstraction.

This last stage of general education destined to give the pupil a comprehensive and connected view of the things which he has already learnt separately, includes a philosophic study of the Methods of the sciences; the modes in which the human intellect proceeds from the known to the unknown. We must be taught to generalize our conception of the resources which the human mind possesses for the exploration of nature; to understand how man discovers the real facts of the world, and by what tests he can judge whether he has really found them. And doubtless this is the crown and consummation of a liberal education: but before we restrict an University to this highest department of instruction—before we confine it to teaching, not knowledge, but the philosophy of knowledge—we must be assured that the knowledge itself has been acquired elsewhere. Those who take this view of the function of an University are not wrong in thinking that the schools, as distinguished from the universities, ought to be adequate to teaching every branch of general instruction required by youth, so far as it can be studied apart from the rest. But where are such schools to be found? Since science assumed its modern character, nowhere: and in these islands less even than elsewhere. This ancient kingdom, thanks to its great religious reformers, had the inestimable advantage, denied to its southern sister, of excellent parish schools, which gave, really and not in pretence, a considerable amount of valuable literary instruction to the bulk of the population, two centuries earlier than in any other country. But schools of a still higher description have been, even in Scotland, so few and inadequate, that the Universities have had to perform largely the functions which ought to be performed by schools; receiving students at an early age, and undertaking not only the work for which the schools should have prepared them, but much of the preparation itself. Every Scottish University is not an University only, but a High School, to supply the deficiency of other schools. And if the English Universities do not do the same, it is not because the same need does not exist, but because it is disregarded. Youths come to the Scottish Universities ignorant, and are there taught. The majority of those who come to the English Universities come still more ignorant, and ignorant they go away.

In point of fact, therefore, the office of a Scottish University comprises the whole of a liberal education, from the foundations upwards. And the scheme of your Universities has, almost from the beginning, really aimed at including the whole, both in depth and in breadth. You have not, as the English Universities so long did, confined all the stress of your teaching, all your real effort to teach, within the limits of two subjects, the classical languages and mathematics. You did not wait till the last few years to establish a Natural Science and a Moral Science Tripos. Instruction in both those departments was organized long ago: and your teachers of those subjects have not been nominal professors, who did not lecture: some of the greatest names in physical and in moral science have taught in your Universities, and by their teaching contributed to form some of the most distinguished intellects of the last and present centuries. To comment upon the course of education at the Scottish Universities is to pass in review every essential department of general culture. The best use, then, which I am able to make of the present occasion, is to offer a few remarks on each of those departments, considered in its relation to human cultivation at large: adverting to the nature of the claims which each has to a place in liberal education; in what special manner they each conduce to the improvement of the individual mind and the benefit of the race; and how they all conspire to the common end, the strengthening, exalting, purifying, and beautifying of our common nature, and the fitting out of mankind with the necessary mental implements for the work they have to perform through life.

Let me first say a few words on the great controversy of
the present day with regard to the higher education, the
difference which most broadly divides educational reformers
and conservatives; the vexed question between the ancient
languages and the modern sciences and arts; whether
general education should be classical—let me use a wider
expression, and say literary—or scientific. A dispute as
endlessly, and often as fruitlessly agitated as that old controversy which it resembles, made memorable by the names
of Swift and Sir William Temple in England and Fon-
tenelle in France—the contest for superiority between the
ancients and the moderns. This question, whether we
should be taught the classics or the sciences, seems to me,
I confess, very like a dispute whether painters should
cultivate drawing or colouring, or, to use a more homely
illustration, whether a tailor should make coats or trousers.
I can only reply by the question, why not both? Can
anything deserve the name of a good education which does
not include literature and science too? If there were no
more to be said than that scientific education teaches us to
think, and literary education to express our thoughts, do
we not require both? and is not any one a poor, maimed,
lopsided fragment of humanity who is deficient in either?
We are not obliged to ask ourselves whether it is more
important to know the languages or the sciences. Short as
life is, and shorter still as we make it by the time we waste
on things which are neither business, nor meditation, nor
pleasure, we are not so badly off that our scholars need be
ignorant of the laws and properties of the world they live
in, or our scientific men destitute of poetic feeling and
artistic cultivation. I am amazed at the limited conception
which many educational reformers have formed to themselves of a human being's power of acquisition. The study
of science, they truly say, is indispensable: our present

education neglects it: there is truth in this too, though it is not all truth: and they think it impossible to find room for the studies which they desire to encourage, but by turning out, at least from general education, those which are now chiefly cultivated. How absurd, they say, that the whole of boyhood should be taken up in acquiring an imperfect knowledge of two dead languages. Absurd indeed: but is the human mind's capacity to learn, measured by that of Eton and Westminster to teach? I should prefer to see these reformers pointing their attacks against the shameful inefficiency of the schools, public and private, which pretend to teach these two languages and do not. I should like to hear them denounce the wretched methods of teaching, and the criminal idleness and supineness, which waste the entire boyhood of the pupils without really giving to most of them more than a smattering, if even that, of the only kind of knowledge which is even pretended to be cared for. Let us try what conscientious and intelligent teaching can do, before we presume to decide what cannot be done.

Scotland has on the whole, in this respect, been considerably more fortunate than England. Scotch youths have never found it impossible to leave school or the university having learnt somewhat of other things besides Greek and Latin; and why? Because Greek and Latin have been better taught. A beginning of classical instruction has all along been made in the common schools: and the common schools of Scotland, like her Universities, have never been the mere shams that the English Universities were during the last century, and the greater part of the English classical schools still are. The only tolerable Latin grammars for school purposes that I know of, which had been produced in these islands until very lately, were written by Scotchmen. Reason, indeed, is beginning to find its way by gradual infiltration even into English schools, and to maintain a contest, though as yet a very unequal one, against routine. A few practical reformers of school tuition, of whom Arnold was the most eminent, have made a beginning of amendment in many things: but reforms, worthy of the name, are always slow, and reform even of governments and churches is not so slow as that of schools, for there is the great preliminary difficulty of fashioning the instruments: of teaching the teachers. If all the improvements in the mode of teaching languages which are already sanctioned by experience, were adopted into our classical schools, we should soon cease to hear of Latin and Greek as studies which must engross the school years, and render impossible any other acquirements. If a boy learnt Greek and Latin on the same principle on which a mere child learns with such ease and rapidity any modern language, namely, by 'acquiring some familiarity with the vocabulary by practice and repetition, before being troubled with grammatical rules—those rules being acquired with tenfold greater facility when the cases to which they apply are already familiar to the mind; an average schoolboy, long before the age at which schooling terminates, would be able to read fluently and with intelligent interest any ordinary Latin or Greek author in prose or verse, would have a competent knowledge of the grammatical structure of both languages, and have had time besides for an ample amount of scientific instruction. I might go much further; but I am as unwilling to speak out all that I think practicable in this matter, as George Stephenson was about railways, when he calculated the average speed of a train at ten miles an hour, because if he had estimated it higher, the practical men would have turned a deaf ear to him, as that most unsafe character in their estimation, an enthusiast and a visionary. The results have shewn, in that case, who was the real practical man. What the results would shew in the other case, I will not attempt to anticipate. But I will say confidently, that if the two classical languages were properly taught, there would be no need whatever for ejecting them from the school course, in order to have sufficient time for everything else that need be included therein.

Let me say a few words more on this strangely limited estimate of what it is possible for human beings to learn, resting on a tacit assumption that they are already as efficiently taught as they ever can be. So narrow a conception not only vitiates our idea of education, but actually, if we receive it, darkens our anticipations as to the future progress of mankind. For if the inexorable conditions of human life make it useless for one man to attempt to know more than one thing, what is to become of the human intellect as facts accumulate? In every generation, and now more rapidly than ever, the things which it is necessary that somebody should know are more and more multiplied. Every department of knowledge becomes so loaded with details, that one who endeavours to know it with minute accuracy, must confine himself to a smaller and smaller portion of the whole extent: every science and art must be cut up into subdivisions, until each man's portion, the district which he thoroughly knows, bears about the same ratio to the whole range of useful knowledge that the art of putting on a pin's head does to the field of human industry. Now, if in order to know that little completely, it is necessary to remain wholly ignorant of all the rest, what will soon be the worth of a man, for any human purpose except his own infinitesimal fraction of human wants and requirements? His state will be even worse than that of simple ignorance. Experience proves that there is no one study or pursuit, which, practised to the exclusion of all others, does not narrow and pervert the mind; breeding in it a class of prejudices special to that pursuit, besides a general prejudice, common to all narrow specialities, against large views, from an incapacity to take in and appreciate the grounds of them. We should have to expect that human nature would be more and more dwarfed, and unfitted for great things, by its very proficiency in small ones. But matters are not so bad with us: there is no ground for so dreary an anticipation. It is not the utmost limit of human acquirement to know only one thing, but to combine a minute knowledge of one or a few things with a general knowledge of many things. By a general knowledge I do not mean a few vague impressions. An eminent man, one of whose writings is part of the course of this University, Archbishop Whately, has well discriminated between a general knowledge and a superficial knowledge. To have a general knowledge of a subject is to know only its leading truths, but to know these not superficially but thoroughly, so as to have a true conception of the subject in its great features; leaving the minor details to those who require them for the purposes of their special pursuit. There is no incompatibility between knowing a wide range of subjects up to this point, and some one subject with the completeness required by those who make it their principal occupation. It is this combination which gives an enlightened public: a body of cultivated intellects, each taught by its attainments in its own province what real knowledge is, and knowing enough of other subjects to be able to discern who are those that know them better. The amount of knowledge is not to be lightly estimated, which qualifies us for judging to whom we may have recourse for more. The elements of the more important studies being widely diffused, those who have reached the higher summits find a public capable of appreciating their

superiority, and prepared to follow their lead. It is thus too
that minds are formed capable of guiding and improving
public opinion on the greater concerns of practical life.
Government and civil society are the most complicated of
all subjects accessible to the human mind: and he who
would deal competently with them as a thinker, and not
as a blind follower of a party, requires not only a general
knowledge of the leading facts of life, both moral and
material, but an understanding exercised and disciplined in
the principles and rules of sound thinking, up to a point
which neither the experience of life, nor any one science
or branch of knowledge, affords. Let us understand, then,
that it should be our aim in learning, not merely to know
the one thing which is to be our principal occupation, as
well as it can be known, but to do this and also to know
something of all the great subjects of human interest:
taking care to know that something accurately; marking
well the dividing line between what we know accurately
and what we do not: and remembering that our object
should be to obtain a true view of nature and life in their
broad outline, and that it is idle to throw away time upon
the details of anything which is to form no part of the
occupation of our practical energies.

It by no means follows, however, that every useful
branch of general, as distinct from professional, knowledge,
should be included in the curriculum of school or university
studies. There are things which are better learnt out of
school, or when the school years, and even those usually
passed in a Scottish university, are over. I do not agree
with those reformers who would give a regular and prominent place in the school or university course to modern
languages. This is not because I attach small importance
to the knowledge of them. No one can in our age be
esteemed a well-instructed person who is not familiar with

at least the French language, so as to read French books with ease; and there is great use in cultivating a familiarity with German. But living languages are so much more easily acquired by intercourse with those who use them in daily life; a few months in the country itself, if properly employed, go so much farther than as many years of school lessons; that it is really waste of time for those to whom that easier mode is attainable, to labour at them with no help but that of books and masters: and it will in time be made attainable, through international schools and colleges, to many more than at present. Universities do enough to facilitate the study of modern languages, if they give a mastery over that ancient language which is the foundation of most of them, and the possession of which makes it easier to learn four or five of the continental languages than it is to learn one of them without it. Again, it has always seemed to me a great absurdity that history and geography should be taught in schools; except in elementary schools for the children of the labouring classes, whose subsequent access to books is limited. Who ever really learnt history and geography except by private reading? and what an utter failure a system of education must be, if it has not given the pupil a sufficient taste for reading to seek for himself those most attractive and easily intelligible of all kinds of knowledge? Besides, such history and geography as can be taught in schools exercise none of the faculties of the intelligence except the memory. An University is indeed the place where the student should be introduced to the Philosophy of History; where Professors who not merely know the facts but have exercised their minds on them, should initiate him into the causes and explanation, so far as within our reach, of the past life of mankind in its principal features. Historical criticism also—the tests of historical truth—are a subject to which his attention may well be drawn in this stage of his education. But of the mere facts of history, as commonly accepted, what educated youth of any mental activity does not learn as much as is necessary, if he is simply turned loose into an historical library? What he needs on this, and on most other matters of common information, is not that he should be taught it in boyhood, but that abundance of books should be accessible to him.

The only languages, then, and the only literature, to which I would allow a place in the ordinary curriculum, are those of the Greeks and Romans; and to these I would preserve the position in it which they at present occupy. That position is justified, by the great value, in education, of knowing well some other cultivated language and literature than one's own, and by the peculiar value of those particular languages and literatures.

There is one purely intellectual benefit from a knowledge of languages, which I am specially desirous to dwell on. Those who have seriously reflected on the causes of human error, have been deeply impressed with the tendency of mankind to mistake words for things. Without entering into the metaphysics of the subject, we know how common it is to use words glibly and with apparent propriety, and to accept them confidently when used by others, without ever having had any distinct conception of the things denoted by them. To quote again from Archbishop Whately, it is the habit of mankind to mistake familiarity for accurate knowledge. As we seldom think of asking the meaning of what we see every day, so when our ears are used to the sound of a word or a phrase, we do not suspect that it conveys no clear idea to our minds, and that we should have the utmost difficulty in defining it, or expressing, in any other words, what we think we understand by it. Now it is obvious in what manner this bad habit tends to be corrected by the practice of translating with accuracy from one language to another, and hunting out the meanings expressed in a vocabulary with which we have not grown familiar by early and constant use. I hardly know any greater proof of the extraordinary genius of the Greeks, than that they were able to make such brilliant achievements in abstract thought, knowing, as they generally did, no language but their own. But the Greeks did not escape the effects of this deficiency. Their greatest intellects, those who laid the foundation of philosophy and of all our intellectual culture, Plato and Aristotle, are con- tinually led away by words; mistaking the accidents of language for real relations in nature, and supposing that things which have the same name in the Greek tongue must be the same in their own essence. There is a well- known saying of Hobbes, the far-reaching significance of which you will more and more appreciate in proportion to the growth of your own intellect: "Words are the counters of wise men, but the money of fools." With the wise man a word stands for the fact which it represents; to the fool it is itself the fact. To carry on Hobbes' metaphor, the counter is far more likely to be taken for merely what it is, by those who are in the habit of using many different kinds of counters. But besides the advantage of possessing another cultivated language, there is a further consideration equally important. Without knowing the language of a people, we never really know their thoughts, their feelings, and their type of character: and unless we do possess this knowledge, of some other people than ourselves, we remain, to the hour of our death, with our intellects only half expanded. Look at a youth who has never been out of his family circle: he never dreams of any other opinions or ways of thinking than those he has been bred up in; or, if he has heard of any such, attributes them to some moral defect, or inferiority of nature or education. If his family are Tory, he cannot conceive the possibility of being a Liberal; if Liberal, of being a Tory. What the notions and habits of a single family are to a boy who has had no intercourse beyond it, the notions and habits of his own country are to him who is ignorant of every other. Those notions and habits are to him human nature itself; whatever varies from them is an unaccountable aberration which he cannot mentally realize: the idea that any other ways can be right, or as near an approach to right as some of his own, is inconceivable to him. This does not merely close his eyes to the many things which every country still has to learn from others: it hinders every country from reaching the improvement which it could otherwise attain by itself. We are not likely to correct any of our opinions or mend any of our ways, unless we begin by conceiving that they are capable of amendment: but merely to know that foreigners think differently from ourselves, without understanding why they do so, or what they really do think, does but confirm us in our self-conceit, and connect our national vanity with the preservation of our own peculiarities. Improvement consists in bringing our opinions into nearer agreement with facts; and we shall not be likely to do this while we look at facts only through glasses coloured by those very opinions. But since we cannot divest ourselves of preconceived notions, there is no known means of eliminating their influence but by frequently using the differently coloured glasses of other people: and those of other nations, as the most different, are the best.

But if it is so useful, on this account, to know the language and literature of any other cultivated and civilized people, the most valuable of all to us in this respect are the languages and literature of the ancients. No nations of modern and civilized Europe are so unlike one another, as the Greeks and Romans are unlike all of us; yet without being, as some remote Orientals are, so totally dissimilar, that the labour of a life is required to enable us to understand them. Were this the only gain to be derived from a knowledge of the ancients, it would already place the study of them in a high rank among enlightening and liberalizing pursuits. It is of no use saying that we may know them through modern writings. We may know something of them in that way; which is much better than knowing nothing. But modern books do not teach us ancient thought; they teach us some modern writer's notion of ancient thought. Modern books do not shew us the Greeks and Romans; they tell us some modern writer's opinions about the Greeks and Romans. Translations are scarcely better. When we want really to know what a person thinks or says, we seek it at first hand from himself. We do not trust to another person's impression of his meaning, given in another person's words; we refer to his own. Much more is it necessary to do so when his words are in one language, and those of his reporter in another. Modern phraseology never conveys the exact meaning of a Greek writer; it cannot do so, except by a diffuse explanatory circumlocution which no translator dares use. We must be able, in a certain degree, to think in Greek, if we would represent to ourselves how a Greek thought: and this not only in the abstruse region of metaphysics, but about the political, religious, and even domestic concerns of life. I will mention a further aspect of this question, which, though I have not the merit of originating it, I do not remember to have seen noticed in any book. There is no part of our knowledge which it is more useful to obtain at first hand—to go to the fountain head for—than our knowledge of history. Yet this, in most cases, we hardly ever do. Our conception of the past is not drawn from its own

records, but from books written about it, containing not
the facts, but a view of the facts which has shaped itself in
the mind of somebody of our own or a very recent time.
Such books are very instructive and valuable; they help us
to understand history, to interpret history, to draw just
conclusions from it; at the worst, they set us the example
of trying to do all this; but they are not themselves
history. The knowledge they give is upon trust, and even
when they have done their best, it is not only incomplete
but partial, because confined to what a few modern writers
have seen in the materials, and have thought worth picking
out from among them. How little we learn of our own
ancestors from Hume, or Hallam, or Macaulay, compared
with what we know if we add to what these tell us, even
a little reading of cotemporary authors and documents!
The most recent historians are so well aware of this, that
they fill their pages with extracts from the original materials, feeling that these extracts are the real history, and
their comments and thread of narrative are only helps towards understanding it. Now it is part of the great worth
to us of our Greek and Latin studies, that in them we do
read history in the original sources. We are in actual contact with cotemporary minds; we are not dependent on
hearsay; we have something by which we can test and
check the representations and theories of modern historians.
It may be asked, why then not study the original materials
of modern history? I answer, it is highly desirable to do
so; and let me remark by the way, that even this requires
a dead language; nearly all the documents prior to the
Reformation, and many subsequent to it, being written in
Latin. But the exploration of these documents, though a
most useful pursuit, cannot be a branch of education. Not
to speak of their vast extent, and the fragmentary nature
of each, the strongest reason is, that in learning the spirit

of our own past ages, until a comparatively recent period, from cotemporary writers, we learn hardly anything else. Those authors, with a few exceptions, are little worth reading on their own account. While, in studying the great writers of antiquity, we are not only learning to understand the ancient mind, but laying in a stock of wise thought and observation, still valuable to ourselves; and at the same time making ourselves familiar with a number of the most perfect and finished literary compositions which the human mind has produced—compositions which, from the altered conditions of human life, are likely to be seldom paralleled, in their sustained excellence, by the times to come.

Even as mere languages, no modern European language is so valuable a discipline to the intellect as those of Greece and Rome, on account of their regular and complicated structure. Consider for a moment what grammar is. It is the most elementary part of logic. It is the beginning of the analysis of the thinking process. The principles and rules of grammar are the means by which the forms of language are made to correspond with the universal forms of thought. The distinctions between the various parts of speech, between the cases of nouns, the moods and tenses of verbs, the functions of particles, are distinctions in thought, not merely in words. Single nouns and verbs express objects and events, many of which can be cognized by the senses: but the modes of putting nouns and verbs together, express the relations of objects and events, which can be cognized only by the intellect; and each different mode corresponds to a different relation. The structure of every sentence is a lesson in logic. The various rules of syntax oblige us to distinguish between the subject and predicate of a proposition, between the agent, the action, and the thing acted upon; to mark when an idea is intended to modify or qualify, or merely to unite with, some other idea; what assertions are categorical, what only conditional; whether the intention is to express similarity or contrast, to make a plurality of assertions conjunctively or disjunctively; what portions of a sentence, though grammatically complete within themselves, are mere members or subordinate parts of the assertion made by the entire sentence. Such things form the subject-matter of universal grammar; and the languages which teach it best are those which have the most definite rules, and which provide distinct forms for the greatest number of distinctions in thought, so that if we fail to attend precisely and accurately to any of these, we cannot avoid committing a solecism in language. In these qualities the classical languages have an incomparable superiority over every modern language, and over all languages, dead or living, which have a literature worth being generally studied.

But the superiority of the literature itself, for purposes of education, is still more marked and decisive. Even in the substantial value of the matter of which it is the vehicle, it is very far from having been superseded. The discoveries of the ancients in science have been greatly surpassed, and as much of them as is still valuable loses nothing by being incorporated in modern treatises: but what does not so well admit of being transferred bodily, and has been very imperfectly carried off even piecemeal, is the treasure which they accumulated of what may be called the wisdom of life: the rich store of experience of human nature and conduct, which the acute and observing minds of those ages, aided in their observations by the greater simplicity of manners and life, consigned to their writings, and most of which retains all its value. The speeches in Thucydides, the *Rhetoric*, *Ethics*, and *Politics* of Aristotle; the *Dialogues* of Plato; the *Orations* of Demosthenes; the *Satires*, and especially the *Epistles* of Horace; all the writings of Tacitus;

the great work of Quintilian, a repertory of the best thoughts of the ancient world on all subjects connected with education; and, in a less formal manner, all that is left to us of the ancient historians, orators, philosophers, and even dramatists, are replete with remarks and maxims of singular good sense and penetration, applicable both to political and to private life: and the actual truths we find in them are even surpassed in value by the encouragement and help they give us in the pursuit of truth. Human invention has never produced anything so valuable, in the way both of stimulation and of discipline to the inquiring intellect, as the dialectics of the ancients, of which many of the works of Aristotle illustrate the theory, and those of Plato exhibit the practice. No modern writings come near to these, in teaching, both by precept and example, the way to investigate truth, on those subjects, so vastly important to us, which remain matters of controversy, from the difficulty or impossibility of bringing them to a directly experimental test. To question all things; never to turn away from any difficulty; to accept no doctrine either from ourselves or from other people without a rigid scrutiny by negative criticism, letting no fallacy, or incoherence, or confusion of thought, slip by unperceived; above all, to insist upon having the meaning of a word clearly understood before using it, and the meaning of a proposition before assenting to it; these are the lessons we learn from the ancient dialecticians. With all this vigorous management of the negative element, they inspire no scepticism about the reality of truth, or indifference to its pursuit. The noblest enthusiasm, both for the search after truth and for applying it to its highest uses, pervades these writers, Aristotle no less than Plato, though Plato has incomparably the greater power of imparting those feelings to others. In cultivating, therefore, the ancient languages as our best

literary education, we are all the while laying an admirable foundation for ethical and philosophical culture.
In purely literary excellence—in perfection of form—the
pre-eminence of the ancients is not disputed. In every
department which they attempted, and they attempted
almost all, their composition, like their sculpture, has been
to the greatest modern artists an example, to be looked up
to with hopeless admiration, but of inappreciable value as
a light on high, guiding their own endeavours. In prose
and in poetry, in epic, lyric, or dramatic, as in historical,
philosophical, and oratorical art, the pinnacle on which
they stand is equally eminent. I am now speaking of the
form, the artistic perfection of treatment: for, as regards substance, I consider modern poetry to be superior to ancient,
in the same manner, though in a less degree, as modern
science: it enters deeper into nature. The feelings of the
modern mind are more various, more complex and manifold,
than those of the ancients ever were. The modern mind is,
what the ancient mind was not, brooding and self-conscious;
and its meditative self-consciousness has discovered depths
in the human soul which the Greeks and Romans did not
dream of, and would not have understood. But what they
had got to express, they expressed in a manner which few
even of the greatest moderns have seriously attempted to
rival. It must be remembered that they had more time,
and that they wrote chiefly for a select class, possessed of
leisure. To us who write in a hurry for people who read
in a hurry, the attempt to give an equal degree of finish
would be loss of time. But to be familiar with perfect
models is not the less important to us because the element
in which we work precludes even the effort to equal them.
They shew us at least what excellence is, and make us
desire it, and strive to get as near to it as is within our reach.
And this is the value to us of the ancient writers, all the

more emphatically, because their excellence does not admit
of being copied, or directly imitated. It does not consist in
a trick which can be learnt, but in the perfect adaptation
of means to ends. The secret of the style of the great Greek
and Roman authors, is that it is the perfection of good sense.
In the first place, they never use a word without a meaning,
or a word which adds nothing to the meaning. They always
(to begin with) had a meaning; they knew what they
wanted to say; and their whole purpose was to say it with
the highest degree of exactness and completeness, and bring
it home to the mind with the greatest possible clearness
and vividness. It never entered into their thoughts to conceive of a piece of writing as beautiful in itself, abstractedly
from what it had to express: its beauty must all be subservient to the most perfect expression of the sense. The
curiosa felicitas which their critics ascribed in a pre-eminent
degree to Horace, expresses the standard at which they all
aimed. Their style is exactly described by Swift's definition,
"the right words in the right places." Look at an oration
of Demosthenes; there is nothing in it which calls attention
to itself as style at all: it is only after a close examination
we perceive that every word is what it should be, and where
it should be, to lead the hearer smoothly and imperceptibly
into the state of mind which the orator wishes to produce.
The perfection of the workmanship is only visible in the
total absence of any blemish or fault, and of anything which
checks the flow of thought and feeling, anything which
even momentarily distracts the mind from the main purpose. But then (as has been well said) it was not the object
of Demosthenes to make the Athenians cry out "What a
splendid speaker!" but to make them say "Let us march
against Philip!" It was only in the decline of ancient
literature that ornament began to be cultivated merely as
ornament. In the time of its maturity, not the merest

epithet was put in because it was thought beautiful in itself; nor even for a merely descriptive purpose, for epithets purely descriptive were one of the corruptions of style which abound in Lucan, for example: the word had no business there unless it brought out some feature which was wanted, and helped to place the object in the light which the purpose of the composition required. These conditions being complied with, then indeed the intrinsic beauty of the means used was a source of additional effect, of which it behoved them to avail themselves, like rhythm and melody of versification. But these great writers knew that ornament for the sake of ornament, ornament which attracts attention to itself, and shines by its own beauties, only does so by calling off the mind from the main object, and thus not only interferes with the higher purpose of human discourse, which ought, and generally professes, to have some matter to communicate, apart from the mere excitement of the moment, but also spoils the perfection of the composition as a piece of fine art, by destroying the unity of effect. This, then, is the first great lesson in composition to be learnt from the classical authors. The second is, not to be prolix. In a single paragraph, Thucydides can give a clear and vivid representation of a battle, such as a reader who has once taken it into his mind can seldom forget. The most powerful and affecting piece of narrative perhaps in all historical literature, is the account of the Sicilian catastrophe in his seventh book, yet how few pages does it fill! The ancients were concise, because of the extreme pains they took with their compositions; almost all moderns are prolix, because they do not. The great ancients could express a thought so perfectly in a few words or sentences, that they did not need to add any more: the moderns, because they cannot bring it out clearly and completely at once, return again and again, heaping sentence upon sentence, each adding a little more elucidation, in hopes that though no single sentence expresses the full meaning, the whole together may give a sufficient notion of it. In this respect I am afraid we are growing worse instead of better, for want of time and patience, and from the necessity we are in of addressing almost all writings to a busy and imperfectly prepared public. The demands of modern life are such—the work to be done, the mass to be worked upon, are so vast, that those who have anything particular to say—who have, as the phrase goes, any message to deliver—cannot afford to devote their time to the production of masterpieces. But they would do far worse than they do, if there had never been masterpieces, or if they had never known them. Early familiarity with the perfect, makes our most imperfect production far less bad than it otherwise would be. To have a high standard of excellence often makes the whole difference of rendering our work good when it would otherwise be mediocre.

For all these reasons I think it important to retain these two languages and literatures in the place they occupy, as a part of liberal education, that is, of the education of all who are not obliged by their circumstances to discontinue their scholastic studies at a very early age. But the same reasons which vindicate the place of classical studies in general education, shew also the proper limitation of them. They should be carried as far as is sufficient to enable the pupil, in after life, to read the great works of ancient literature with ease. Those who have leisure and inclination to make scholarship, or ancient history, or general philology, their pursuit, of course require much more, but there is no room for more in general education. The laborious idleness in which the school-time is wasted away in the English classical schools deserves the severest reprehension. To what purpose should the most precious years

of early life be irreparably squandered in learning to write
bad Latin and Greek verses? I do not see that we are
much the better even for those who end by writing good
ones. I am often tempted to ask the favourites of nature
and fortune, whether all the serious and important work
of the world is done, that their time and energy can be
spared for these *nugæ difficiles*? I am not blind to the utility
of composing in a language, as a means of learning it accurately. I hardly know any other means equally effectual.
But why should not prose composition suffice? What need
is there of original composition at all? if that can be called
original which unfortunate schoolboys, without any
thoughts to express, hammer out on compulsion from mere
memory, acquiring the pernicious habit which a teacher
should consider it one of his first duties to repress, that of
merely stringing together borrowed phrases? The exercise
in composition, most suitable to the requirements of
learners, is that most valuable one, of retranslating from
translated passages of a good author: and to this might be
added, what still exists in many Continental places of education, occasional practice in talking Latin. There would
be something to be said for the time spent in the manu-
facture of verses, if such practice were necessary for the
enjoyment of ancient poetry; though it would be better to
lose that enjoyment than to purchase it at so extravagant
a price. But the beauties of a great poet would be a far
poorer thing than they are, if they only impressed us
through a knowledge of the technicalities of his art. The
poet needed those technicalities: they are not necessary to
us. They are essential for criticizing a poem, but not for
enjoying it. All that is wanted is sufficient familiarity with
the language, for its meaning to reach us without any sense
of effort, and clothed with the associations on which the
poet counted for producing his effect. Whoever has this

familiarity, and a practised ear, can have as keen a relish of the music of Virgil and Horace, as of Gray, or Burns, or Shelley, though he know not the metrical rules of a common Sapphic or Alcaic. I do not say that these rules ought not to be taught, but I would have a class apart for them, and would make the appropriate exercises an optional, not a compulsory part of the school teaching.

Much more might be said respecting classical instruction, and literary cultivation in general, as a part of liberal education. But it is time to speak of the uses of scientific instruction: or rather its indispensable necessity, for it is recommended by every consideration which pleads for any high order of intellectual education at all.

The most obvious part of the value of scientific instruction, the mere information that it gives, speaks for itself. We are born into a world which we have not made; a world whose phenomena take place according to fixed laws, of which we do not bring any knowledge into the world with us. In such a world we are appointed to live, and in it all our work is to be done. Our whole working power depends on knowing the laws of the world—in other words, the properties of the things which we have to work with, and to work among, and to work upon. We may and do rely, for the greater part of this knowledge, on the few who in each department make its acquisition their main business in life. But unless an elementary knowledge of scientific truths is diffused among the public, they never know what is certain and what is not, or who are entitled to speak with authority and who are not: and they either have no faith at all in the testimony of science, or are the ready dupes of charlatans and impostors. They alternate between ignorant distrust, and blind, often misplaced, confidence. Besides, who is there who would not wish to understand the meaning of the common physical facts that take

place under his eye? Who would not wish to know why
a pump raises water, why a lever moves heavy weights,
why-it is hot at the tropics and cold at the poles, why the
moon is sometimes dark and sometimes bright, what is the
cause of the tides? Do we not feel that he who is totally
ignorant of these things, let him be ever so skilled in a
special profession, is not an educated man but an ignoramus?
It is surely no small part of education to put us in intelligent
possession of the most important and most universally interesting facts of the universe, so that the world which
surrounds us may not be a sealed book to us, uninteresting
because unintelligible. This, however, is but the simplest
and most obvious part of the utility of science, and the part
which, if neglected in youth, may be the most easily made
up for afterwards. It is more important to understand the
value of scientific instruction as a training and disciplining
process, to fit the intellect for the proper work of a human
being. Facts are the materials of our knowledge, but the
mind itself is the instrument: and it is easier to acquire
facts, than to judge what they prove, and how, through the
facts which we know, to get to those which we want to
know.

The most incessant occupation of the human intellect
throughout life is the ascertainment of truth. We are always
needing to know what is actually true about something or
other. It is not given to us all to discover great general
truths that are a light to all men and to future generations;
though with a better general education the number of those
who could do so would be far greater than it is. But we
all require the ability to judge between the conflicting
opinions which are offered to us as vital truths; to choose
what doctrines we will receive in the matter of religion,
for example; to judge whether we ought to be Tories,
Whigs, or Radicals, or to what length it is our duty to go

with each; to form a rational conviction on great questions
of legislation and internal policy, and on the manner in
which our country should behave to dependencies and to
foreign nations. And the need we have of knowing how
to discriminate truth, is not confined to the larger truths.
All through life it is our most pressing interest to find out
the truth about all the matters we are concerned with. If
we are farmers we want to find what will truly improve
our soil; if merchants, what will truly influence the markets
of our commodities; if judges, or jurymen, or advocates,
who it was that truly did an unlawful act, or to whom a
disputed right truly belongs. Every time we have to make
a new resolution or alter an old one, in any situation in life,
we shall go wrong unless we know the truth about the
facts on which our resolution depends. Now, however
different these searches for truth may look, and however
unlike they really are in their subject-matter, the methods
of getting at truth, and the tests of truth, are in all cases
much the same. There are but two roads by which truth
can be discovered; observation, and reasoning: observation,
of course, including experiment. We all observe, and we
all reason, and therefore, more or less successfully, we all
ascertain truths: but most of us do it very ill, and could
not get on at all were we not able to fall back on others
who do it better. If we could not do it in any degree, we
should be mere instruments in the hands of those who
could: they would be able to reduce us to slavery. Then
how shall we best learn to do this? By being shewn the
way in which it has already been successfully done. The
processes by which truth is attained, reasoning and observation, have been carried to their greatest known perfection
in the physical sciences. As classical literature furnishes
the most perfect types of the art of expression, so do the
physical sciences those of the art of thinking. Mathe-

matics, and its application to astronomy and natural philosophy, are the most complete example of the discovery of
truths by reasoning; experimental science, of their discovery
by direct observation. In all these cases we know that we
can trust the operation, because the conclusions to which
it has led have been found true by subsequent trial. It is
by the study of these, then, that we may hope to qualify
ourselves for distinguishing truth, in cases where there do
not exist the same ready means of verification.

In what consists the principal and most characteristic
difference between one human intellect and another? In
their ability to judge correctly of evidence. Our direct
perceptions of truth are so limited; we know so few things
by immediate intuition, or, as it used to be called, by simple
apprehension—that we depend for almost all our valuable
knowledge, on evidence external to itself; and most of us
are very unsafe hands at estimating evidence, where an
appeal cannot be made to actual eyesight. The intellectual
part of our education has nothing more important to do,
than to correct or mitigate this almost universal infirmity—
this summary and substance of nearly all purely intellectual
weakness. To do this with effect needs all the resources
which the most perfect system of intellectual training can
command. Those resources, as every teacher knows, are
but of three kinds: first, models, secondly, rules, thirdly,
appropriate practice. The models of the art of estimating
evidence are furnished by science; the rules are suggested
by science; and the study of science is the most fundamental
portion of the practice.

Take in the first instance mathematics. It is chiefly
from mathematics we realize the fact that there actually
is a road to truth by means of reasoning; that anything real,
and which will be found true when tried, can be arrived
at by a mere operation of the mind. The flagrant abuse of

mere reasoning in the days of the schoolmen, when men argued confidently to supposed facts of outward nature without properly establishing their premises, or checking the conclusions by observation, created a prejudice in the modern, and especially in the English mind, against deductive reasoning altogether, as a mode of investigation. The prejudice lasted long, and was upheld by the misunderstood authority of Lord Bacon; until the prodigious applications of mathematics to physical science—to the discovery of the laws of external nature—slowly and tardily restored the reasoning process to the place which belongs to it as a source of real knowledge. Mathematics, pure and applied, are still the great conclusive example of what can be done by reasoning. Mathematics also habituates us to several of the principal precautions for the safety of the process. Our first studies in geometry teach us two invaluable lessons. One is, to lay down at the beginning, in express and clear terms, all the premises from which we intend to reason. The other is, to keep every step in the reasoning distinct and separate from all the other steps, and to make each step safe before proceeding to another; expressly stating to ourselves, at every joint in the reasoning, what new premise we there introduce. It is not necessary that we should do this at all times, in all our reasonings. But we must be always able and ready to do it. If the validity of our argument is denied, or if we doubt it ourselves, that is the way to check it. In this way we are often enabled to detect at once the exact place where paralogism or confusion get in: and after sufficient practice we may be able to keep them out from the beginning. It is to mathematics, again, that we owe our first notion of a connected body of truth; truths which grow out of one another, and hang together so that each implies all the rest; that no one of them can be questioned without contra-

dicting another or others, until in the end it appears that
no part of the system can be false unless the whole is so.
Pure mathematics first gave us this conception; applied
mathematics extends it to the realm of physical nature.
Applied mathematics shews us that not only the truths of
abstract number and extension, but the external facts of
the universe, which we apprehend by our senses, form, at
least in a large part of all nature, a web similarly held together. We are able, by reasoning from a few fundamental
truths, to explain and predict the phenomena of material
objects: and what is still more remarkable, the fundamental
truths were themselves found out by reasoning; for they
are not such as are obvious to the senses, but had to be
inferred by a mathematical process from a mass of minute
details, which alone came within the direct reach of human
observation. When Newton, in this manner, discovered
the laws of the solar system, he created, for all posterity, the
true idea of science. He gave the most perfect example we
are ever likely to have, of that union of reasoning and
observation, which by means of facts that can be directly
observed, ascends to laws which govern multitudes of other
facts—laws which not only explain and account for what
we see, but give us assurance beforehand of much that we
do not see, much that we never could have found out by
observation, though, having been found out, it is always
verified by the result.

While mathematics, and the mathematical sciences,
supply us with a typical example of the ascertainment of
truth by reasoning; those physical sciences which are not
mathematical, such as chemistry, and purely experimental
physics, shew us in equal perfection the other mode of
arriving at certain truth, by observation, in its most accurate
form, that of experiment. The value of mathematics in a
logical point of view is an old topic with mathematicians,

and has even been insisted on so exclusively as to provoke a counter-exaggeration, of which a well-known essay by Sir William Hamilton is an example: but the logical value of experimental science is comparatively a new subject, yet there is no intellectual discipline more important than that which the experimental sciences afford. Their whole occupation consists in doing well, what all of us, during the whole of life, are engaged in doing, for the most part badly. All men do not affect to be reasoners, but all profess, and really attempt, to draw inferences from experience: yet hardly any one, who has not been a student of the physical sciences, sets out with any just idea of what the process of interpreting experience really is. If a fact has occurred once or oftener, and another fact has followed it, people think they have got an experiment, and are well on the road towards shewing that the one fact is the cause of the other. If they did but know the immense amount of precaution necessary to a scientific experiment; with what sedulous care the accompanying circumstances are contrived and varied, so as to exclude every agency but that which is the subject of the experiment—or, when disturbing agencies cannot be excluded, the minute accuracy with which their influence is calculated and allowed for, in order that the residue may contain nothing but what is due to the one agency under examination; if these things were attended to, people would be much less easily satisfied that their opinions have the evidence of experience; many popular notions and generalizations which are in all mouths, would be thought a great deal less certain than they are supposed to be; but we should begin to lay the foundation of really experimental knowledge, on things which are now the subjects of mere vague discussion, where one side finds as much to say and says it as confidently as another, and each person's opinion is less determined by evidence than by his accidental interest or prepossession. In politics, for instance, it is evident to whoever comes to the study from that of the experimental sciences, that no political conclusions of any value for practice can be arrived at by direct experience. Such specific experience as we can have, serves only to verify, and even that insufficiently, the conclusions of reasoning. Take any active force you please in politics, take the liberties of England, or free trade: how should we know that either of these things conduced to prosperity, if we could discern no tendency in the things themselves to produce it? If we had only the evidence of what is called our experience, such prosperity as we enjoy might be owing to a hundred other causes, and might have been obstructed, not promoted, by these. All true political science is, in one sense of the phrase, *à priori*, being deduced from the tendencies of things, tendencies known either through our general experience of human nature, or as the result of an analysis of the course of history, considered as a progressive evolution. It requires, therefore, the union of induction and deduction, and the mind that is equal to it must have been well disciplined in both. But familiarity with scientific experiment at least does the useful service of inspiring a wholesome scepticism about the conclusions which the mere surface of experience suggests.

The study, on the one hand, of mathematics and its applications, on the other, of experimental science, prepares us for the principal business of the intellect, by the practice of it in the most characteristic cases, and by familiarity with the most perfect and successful models of it. But in great things as in small, examples and models are not sufficient: we want rules as well. Familiarity with the correct use of a language in conversation and writing does not make rules of grammar unnecessary; nor does the amplest knowledge of sciences of reasoning and experiment dispense with rules of logic. We may have heard correct reasonings and seen skilful experiments all our lives—we shall not learn by mere imitation to do the like, unless we pay careful attention to how it is done. It is much easier in these abstract matters, than in purely mechanical ones, to mistake bad work for good. To mark out the difference between them is the province of logic. Logic lays down the general principles and laws of the search after truth; the conditions which, whether recognised or not, must actually have been observed if the mind has done its work rightly. Logic is the intellectual complement of mathematics and physics. Those sciences give the practice, of which Logic is the theory. It declares the principles, rules, and precepts, of which they exemplify the observance.

The science of Logic has two parts; ratiocinative and inductive logic. The one helps to keep us right in reasoning from premises, the other in concluding from observation. Ratiocinative logic is much older than inductive, because reasoning in the narrower sense of the word is an easier process than induction, and the science which works by mere reasoning, pure mathematics, had been carried to a considerable height while the sciences of observation were still in the purely empirical period. The principles of ratiocination, therefore, were the earliest understood and systematized, and the logic of ratiocination is even now suitable to an earlier stage in education than that of induction. The principles of induction cannot be properly understood without some previous study of the inductive sciences: but the logic of reasoning, which was already carried to a high degree of perfection by Aristotle, does not absolutely require even a knowledge of mathematics, but can be sufficiently exemplified and illustrated from the practice of daily life.

Of Logic I venture to say, even if limited to that of

mere ratiocination, the theory of names, propositions, and the syllogism, that there is no part of intellectual education which is of greater value, or whose place can so ill be supplied by anything else. Its uses, it is true, are chiefly negative; its function is, not so much to teach us to go right, as to keep us from going wrong. But in the operations of the intellect it is so much easier to go wrong than right; it is so utterly impossible for even the most vigorous mind to keep itself in the path but by maintaining a vigilant watch against all deviations, and noting all the byways by which it is possible to go astray—that the chief difference between one reasoner and another consists in their less or greater liability to be misled. Logic points out all the possible ways in which, starting from true premises, we may draw false conclusions. By its analysis of the reasoning process, and the forms it supplies for stating and setting forth our reasonings, it enables us to guard the points at which a fallacy is in danger of slipping in, or to lay our fingers upon the place where it has slipped in. When I consider how very simple the theory of reasoning is, and how short a time is sufficient for acquiring a thorough knowledge of its principles and rules, and even considerable expertness in applying them, I can find no excuse for omission to study it on the part of any one who aspires to succeed in any intellectual pursuit. Logic is the great disperser of hazy and confused thinking: it clears up the fogs which hide from us our own ignorance, and make us believe that we understand a subject when we do not. We must not be led away by talk about inarticulate giants who do great deeds without knowing how, and see into the most recondite truths without any of the ordinary helps, and without being able to explain to other people how they reach their conclusions, nor consequently to convince any other people of the truth of them. There may be such men, as there are deaf and dumb persons who do clever things, but for all that, speech and hearing are faculties by no means to be dispensed with. If you want to know whether you are thinking rightly, put your thoughts into words. In the very attempt to do this you will find yourselves, consciously or unconsciously, using logical forms. Logic compels us to throw our meaning into distinct propositions, and our reasonings into distinct steps. It makes us conscious of all the implied assumptions on which we are proceeding, and which, if not true, vitiate the entire process. It makes us aware what extent of doctrine we commit ourselves to by any course of reasoning, and obliges us to look the implied premises in the face, and make up our minds whether we can stand to them. It makes our opinions consistent with themselves and with one another, and forces us to think clearly, even when it cannot make us think correctly. It is true that error may be consistent and systematic as well as truth; but this is not the common case. It is no small advantage to see clearly the principles and consequences involved in our opinions, and which we must either accept, or else abandon those opinions. We are much nearer to finding truth when we search for it in broad daylight. Error, pursued rigorously to all that is implied in it, seldom fails to get detected by coming into collision with some known and admitted fact.

You will find abundance of people to tell you that logic is no help to thought, and that people cannot be taught to think by rules. Undoubtedly rules by themselves, without practice, go but a little way in teaching anything. But if the practice of thinking is not improved by rules, I venture to say it is the only difficult thing done by human beings that is not so. A man learns to saw wood principally by practice, but there are rules for doing it, grounded on the nature of the operation, and if he is not taught the rules, he will not saw well until he has discovered them for himself. Wherever there is a right way and a wrong, there must be a difference between them, and it must be possible to find out what the difference is; and when found out and expressed in words, it is a rule for the operation. If any one is inclined to disparage rules, I say to him, try to learn anything which there are rules for, without knowing the rules, and see how you succeed. To those who think lightly of the school logic, I say, take the trouble to learn it. You will easily do so in a few weeks, and you will see whether it is of no use to you in making your mind clear, and keeping you from stumbling in the dark over the most outrageous fallacies. Nobody, I believe, who has really learnt it, and who goes on using his mind, is insensible to its benefits, unless he started with a prejudice, or, like some eminent English and Scottish thinkers of the past century, is under the influence of a reaction against the exaggerated pretensions made by the schoolmen, not so much in behalf of logic as of the reasoning process itself. Still more highly must the use of logic be estimated, if we include in it, as we ought to do, the principles and rules of Induction as well as of Ratiocination. As the one logic guards us against bad deduction, so does the other against bad generalization, which is a still more universal error. If men easily err in arguing from one general proposition to another, still more easily do they go wrong in interpreting the observations made by themselves and others. There is nothing in which an untrained mind shows itself more hopelessly incapable, than in drawing the proper general conclusions from its own experience. And even trained minds, when all their training is on a special subject, and does not extend to the general principles of induction, are only kept right when there are ready opportunities of verifying their inferences by facts. Able scientific men, when they venture upon subjects in which they have no facts to check them, are often found drawing conclusions or making generalizations from their experimental knowledge, such as any sound theory of induction would shew to be utterly unwarranted. So true is it that practice alone, even of a good kind, is not sufficient without principles and rules. Lord Bacon had the great merit of seeing that rules were necessary, and conceiving, to a very considerable extent, their true character. The defects of his conception were such as were inevitable while the inductive sciences were only in the earliest stage of their progress, and the highest efforts of the human mind in that direction had not yet been made. Inadequate as the Baconian view of induction was, and rapidly as the practice outgrew it, it is only within a generation or two that any considerable improvement has been made in the theory; very much through the impulse given by two of the many distinguished men who have adorned the Scottish universities, Dugald Stewart and Brown.

I have given a very incomplete and summary view of the educational benefits derived from instruction in the more perfect sciences, and in the rules for the proper use of the intellectual faculties which the practice of those sciences has suggested. There are other sciences, which are in a more backward state, and tax the whole powers of the mind in its mature years, yet a beginning of which may be beneficially made in university studies, while a tincture of them is valuable even to those who are never likely to proceed further. The first is physiology; the science of the laws of organic and animal life, and especially of the structure and functions of the human body. It would be absurd to pretend that a profound knowledge of this difficult subject can be acquired in youth, or as a part of general education. Yet an acquaintance with its leading truths is one of those acquirements which ought not to be

the exclusive property of a particular profession. The value
of such knowledge for daily uses has been made familiar
to us all by the sanitary discussions of late years. There is
hardly one among us who may not, in some position of
authority, be required to form an opinion and take part in
public action on sanitary subjects. And the importance of
understanding the true conditions of health and disease—
of knowing how to acquire and preserve that healthy habit
of body which the most tedious and costly medical treatment so often fails to restore when once lost, should secure
a place in general education for the principal maxims of
hygiene, and some of those even of practical medicine.
For those who aim at high intellectual cultivation, the
study of physiology has still greater recommendations, and
is, in the present state of advancement of the higher studies,
a real necessity. The practice which it gives in the study
of nature is such as no other physical science affords in
the same kind, and is the best introduction to the difficult
questions of politics and social life. Scientific education,
apart from professional objects, is but a preparation for
judging rightly of Man, and of his requirements and interests. But to this final pursuit, which has been called
par excellence the proper study of mankind, physiology is
the most serviceable of the sciences, because it is the nearest.
Its subject is already Man: the same complex and manifold
being, whose properties are not independent of circumstance, and immovable from age to age, like those of the
ellipse and hyperbola, or of sulphur and phosphorus, but
are infinitely various, indefinitely modifiable by art or
accident, graduating by the nicest shades into one another,
and reacting upon one another in a thousand ways, so that
they are seldom capable of being isolated and observed
separately. With the difficulties of the study of a being so
constituted, the physiologist, and he alone among scientific

enquirers, is already familiar. Take what view we will of man as a spiritual being, one part of his nature is far more like another than either of them is like anything else. In the organic world we study nature under disadvantages very similar to those which affect the study of moral and political phenomena: our means of making experiments are almost as limited, while the extreme complexity of the facts makes the conclusions of general reasoning unusually precarious, on account of the vast number of circumstances that conspire to determine every result. Yet in spite of these obstacles, it is found possible in physiology to arrive at a considerable number of well-ascertained and important truths. This therefore is an excellent school in which to study the means of overcoming similar difficulties elsewhere. It is in physiology too that we are first introduced to some of the conceptions which play the greatest part in the moral and social sciences, but which do not occur at all in those of inorganic nature. As, for instance, the idea of predisposition, and of predisposing causes, as distinguished from exciting causes. The operation of all moral forces is immensely influenced by predisposition: without that element, it is impossible to explain the commonest facts of history and social life. Physiology is also the first science in which we recognise the influence of habit—the tendency of something to happen again merely because it has happened before. From physiology, too, we get our clearest notion of what is meant by development or evolution. The growth of a plant or animal from the first germ is the typical specimen of a phenomenon which rules through the whole course of the history of man and society —increase of function, through expansion and differentiation of structure by internal forces. I cannot enter into the subject at greater length; it is enough if I throw out hints which may be germs of further thought in yourselves.

Those who aim at high intellectual achievements may be assured that no part of their time will be less wasted, than that which they employ in becoming familiar with the methods and with the main conceptions of the science of organization and life.

Physiology, at its upper extremity, touches on Psychology, or the Philosophy of Mind: and without raising any disputed questions about the limits between Matter and Spirit, the nerves and brain are admitted to have so intimate a connexion with the mental operations, that the student of the last cannot dispense with a considerable knowledge of the first. The value of psychology itself need hardly be expatiated upon in a Scottish university; for it has always been there studied with brilliant success. Almost everything which has been contributed from these islands towards its advancement since Locke and Berkeley, has until very lately, and much of it even in the present generation, proceeded from Scottish authors and Scottish professors. Psychology, in truth, is simply the knowledge of the laws of human nature. If there is anything that deserves to be studied by man, it is his own nature and that of his fellow-men: and if it is worth studying at all, it is worth studying scientifically, so as to reach the fundamental laws which underlie and govern all the rest. With regard to the suitableness of this subject for general education, a distinction must be made. There are certain observed laws of our thoughts and of our feelings which rest upon experimental evidence, and, once seized, are a clue to the interpretation of much that we are conscious of in ourselves, and observe in one another. Such, for example, are the laws of association. Psychology, so far as it consists of such laws—I speak of the laws themselves, not of their disputed applications—is as positive and certain a science as chemistry, and fit to be taught as such. When, however, we pass beyond the bounds of these admitted truths, to questions which are still in controversy among the different philosophical schools— how far the higher operations of the mind can be explained by association, how far we must admit other primary principles—what faculties of the mind are simple, what complex, and what is the composition of the latter—above all, when we embark upon the sea of metaphysics properly so called, and enquire, for instance, whether time and space are real existences, as is our spontaneous impression, or forms of our sensitive faculty, as is maintained by Kant, or complex ideas generated by association; whether matter and spirit are conceptions merely relative to our faculties, or facts existing *per se*, and in the latter case, what is the nature and limit of our knowledge of them; whether the will of man is free or determined by causes, and what is the real difference between the two doctrines; matters on which the most thinking men, and those who have given most study to the subjects, are still divided; it is neither to be expected nor desired that those who do not specially devote themselves to the higher departments of speculation should employ much of their time in attempting to get to the bottom of these questions. But it is a part of liberal education to know that such controversies exist, and, in a general way, what has been said on both sides of them. It is instructive to know the failures of the human intellect as well as its successes, its imperfect as well as its perfect attainments; to be aware of the open questions, as well as of those which have been definitively resolved. A very summary view of these disputed matters may suffice for the many; but a system of education is not intended solely for the many: it has to kindle the aspirations and aid the efforts of those who are destined to stand forth as thinkers above the multitude: and for these there is hardly to be found any discipline comparable to that which these metaphysical controversies afford. For they are essentially questions about the estimation of evidence; about the ultimate grounds of belief; the conditions required to justify our most familar and intimate convictions; and the real meaning and import of words and phrases which we have used from infancy as if we understood all about them, which are even at the foundation of human language, yet of which no one except a metaphysician has rendered to himself a complete account. Whatever philosophical opinions the study of these questions may lead us to adopt, no one ever came out of the discussion of them without increased vigour of understanding, an increased demand for precision of thought and language, and a more careful and exact appreciation of the nature of proof. There never was any sharpener of the intellectual faculties superior to the Berkeleian controversy. There is even now no reading more profitable to students—confining myself to writers in our own language, and notwithstanding that so many of their speculations are already obsolete—than Hobbes and Locke, Reid and Stewart, Hume, Hartley, and Brown: on condition that these great thinkers are not read passively, as masters to be followed, but actively, as supplying materials and incentives to thought. To come to our own cotemporaries, he who has mastered Sir William Hamilton and your own lamented Ferrier as distinguished representatives of one of the two great schools of philosophy, and an eminent Professor in a neighbouring University, Professor Bain, probably the greatest living authority in the other, has gained a practice in the most searching methods of philosophic investigation applied to the most arduous subjects, which is no inadequate preparation for any intellectual difficulties that he is ever likely to be called on to resolve.

In this brief outline of a complete scientific education, I have said nothing about direct instruction in that which it is the chief of all the ends of intellectual education to qualify us for—the exercise of thought on the great interests of mankind as moral and social beings—ethics and politics, in the largest sense. These things are not, in the existing state of human knowledge, the subject of a science, generally admitted and accepted. Politics cannot be learnt once for all, from a text-book, or the instructions of a master. What we require to be taught on that subject, is to be our own teachers. It is a subject on which we have no masters to follow; each must explore for himself, and exercise an independent judgment. Scientific politics do not consist in having a set of conclusions ready made, to be applied everywhere indiscriminately, but in setting the mind to work in a scientific spirit to discover in each instance the truths applicable to the given case. And this, at present, scarcely any two persons do in the same way. Education is not entitled, on this subject, to recommend any set of opinions as resting on the authority of established science. But it can supply the student with materials for his own mind, and helps to use them. It can make him acquainted with the best speculations on the subject, taken from different points of view: none of which will be found complete, while each embodies some considerations really relevant, really requiring to be taken into the account. Education may also introduce us to the principal facts which have a direct bearing on the subject, namely the different modes or stages of civilization that have been found among mankind, and the characteristic properties of each. This is the true purpose of historical studies, as prosecuted in an University. The leading facts of ancient and modern history should be known by the student from his private reading: if that knowledge be wanting, it cannot possibly be supplied here. What a Professor of History has to teach, is the meaning of those facts. His office is to help the student in collecting from history what are the main differences between human beings, and between the institutions of society, at one time or place and at another: in picturing to himself human life and the human conception of life, as they were at the different stages of human development: in distinguishing between what is the same in all ages and what is progressive, and forming some incipient conception of the causes and laws of progress. All these things are as yet very imperfectly understood even by the most philosophic enquirers, and are quite unfit to be taught dogmatically. The object is to lead the student to attend to them; to make. him take interest in history not as a mere narrative, but as a chain of causes and effects still unwinding itself before his eyes, and full of momentous consequences to himself and his descendants; the unfolding of a great epic or dramatic action, to terminate in the happiness or misery, the elevation or degradation, of the human race; an unremitting conflict between good and evil powers, of which every act done by any of us, insignificant as we are, forms one of the incidents; a conflict in which even the smallest of us cannot escape from taking part, in which whoever does not help the right side is helping the wrong, and for our share in which, whether it be greater or smaller, and let its actual consequences be visible or in the main invisible, no one of us can escape the responsibility. Though education cannot arm and equip its pupils for this fight with any complete philosophy either of politics or of history, there is much positive instruction that it can give them, having a direct bearing on the duties of citizenship. They should be taught the outlines of the civil and political institutions of their own country, and in a more general way, of the more advanced of the other civilized nations. Those branches of politics, or of the laws of social life, in which there exists a collection of facts or thoughts sufficiently sifted and methodized to form the beginning of a science, should be taught *ex professo*. Among the chief of these is Political Economy; the sources and conditions of wealth and material prosperity for aggregate bodies of human beings. This study approaches nearer to the rank of a science, in the sense in which we apply that name to the physical sciences, than anything else connected with politics yet does. I need not enlarge on the important lessons which it affords for the guidance of life, and for the estimation of laws and institutions, or on the necessity of knowing all that it can teach in order to have true views of the course of human affairs, or form plans for their improvement which will stand actual trial. The same persons who cry down Logic will generally warn you against Political Economy. It is unfeeling, they will tell you. It recognises unpleasant facts. For my part, the most unfeeling thing I know of is the law of gravitation: it breaks the neck of the best and most amiable person without scruple, if he forgets for a single moment to give heed to it. The winds and waves too are very unfeeling. Would you advise those who go to sea to deny the winds and waves—or to make use of them, and find the means of guarding against their dangers? My advice to you is to study the great writers on Political Economy, and hold firmly by whatever in them you find true; and depend upon it that if you are not selfish or hard-hearted already, Political Economy will not make you so. Of no less importance than Political Economy is the study of what is called Jurisprudence; the general principles of law; the social necessities which laws are required to meet; the features common to all systems of law, and the differences between them; the requisites of good legislation, the proper mode of constructing a legal system, and the best constitution of courts of justice and modes of legal procedure. These things are not only the chief part of the business of government, but the vital concern of every citizen; and their improvement affords a wide scope for the energies of any duly prepared mind, ambitious of contributing towards the better condition of the human race. For this, too, admirable helps have been provided by writers of our own or of a very recent time. At the head of them stands Bentham; undoubtedly the greatest master who ever devoted the labour of a life to let in light on the subject of law; and who is the more intelligible to non-professional persons, because, as his way is, he builds up the subject from its foundation in the facts of human life, and shows by careful consideration of ends and means, what law might and ought to be, in deplorable contrast with what it is. Other enlightened jurists have followed with contributions of two kinds, as the type of which I may take two works, equally admirable in their respective times. Mr. Austin, in his *Lectures on Jurisprudence*, takes for his basis the Roman law, the most elaborately consistent legal system which history has shewn us in actual operation, and that which the greatest number of accomplished minds have employed themselves in harmonizing. From this he singles out the principles and distinctions which are of general applicability, and employs the powers and resources of a most precise and analytic mind to give to those principles and distinctions a philosophic basis, grounded in the universal reason of mankind, and not in mere technical convenience. Mr. Maine, in his treatise on *Ancient Law in its relations to Modern Thought*, shews from the history of law, and from what is known of the primitive institutions of mankind, the origin of much that has lasted till now, and has a firm footing both in the laws and in the ideas of modern times; shewing that many of these things never originated in reason, but are relics of the institutions of barbarous society,

modified more or less by civilization, but kept standing by
the persistency of ideas which were the offspring of those
barbarous institutions, and have survived their parent. The
path opened by Mr. Maine has been followed up by others,
with additional illustrations of the influence of obsolete
ideas on modern institutions, and of obsolete institutions
on modern ideas; an action and reaction which perpetuate,
in many of the greatest concerns, a mitigated barbarism:
things being continually accepted as dictates of nature and
necessities of life, which, if we knew all, we should see to
have originated in artificial arrangements of society, long
since abandoned and condemned.

To these studies I would add International Law; which
I decidedly think should be taught in all universities, and
should form part of all liberal education. The need of it
is far from being limited to diplomatists and lawyers; it
extends to every citizen. What is called the Law of Nations
is not properly law, but a part of ethics: a set of moral rules,
accepted as authoritative by civilized states. It is true that
these rules neither are nor ought to be of eternal obligation,
but do and must vary more or less from age to age, as the
consciences of nations become more enlightened and the
exigencies of political society undergo change. But the
rules mostly were at their origin, and still are, an application of the maxims of honesty and humanity to the intercourse of states. They were introduced by the moral
sentiments of mankind, or by their sense of the general
interest, to mitigate the crimes and sufferings of a state of
war, and to restrain governments and nations from unjust
or dishonest conduct towards one another in time of peace.
Since every country stands in numerous and various relations with the other countries of the world, and many, our
own among the number, exercise actual authority over
some of these, a knowledge of the established rules of

international morality is essential to the duty of every nation, and therefore of every person in it who helps to make up the nation, and whose voice and feeling form a part of what is called public opinion. Let not any one pacify his conscience by the delusion that he can do no harm if he takes no part, and forms no opinion. Bad men need nothing more to compass their ends, than that good men should look on and do nothing. He is not a good man who, without a protest, allows wrong to be committed in his name, and with the means which he helps to supply, because he will not trouble himself to use his mind on the subject. It depends on the habit of attending to and looking into public transactions, and on the degree of information and solid judgment respecting them that exists in the community, whether the conduct of the nation as a nation, both within itself and towards others, shall be selfish, corrupt, and tyrannical, or rational and enlightened, just and noble.

Of these more advanced studies, only a small commencement can be made at schools and universities; but even this is of the highest value, by awakening an interest in the subjects, by conquering the first difficulties, and inuring the mind to the kind of exertion which the studies require, by implanting a desire to make further progress, and directing the student to the best tracks and the best helps. So far as these branches of knowledge have been acquired, we have learnt, or been put into the way of learning, our duty, and our work in life. Knowing it, however, is but half the work of education; it still remains, that what we know, we shall be willing and determined to put in practice. Nevertheless, to know the truth is already a great way towards disposing us to act upon it. What we see clearly and apprehend keenly, we have a natural desire to act out. "To see the best, and yet the worst pursue," is a possible but not a common state of mind; those who follow the

wrong have generally first taken care to be voluntarily
ignorant of the right. They have silenced their conscience,
but they are not knowingly disobeying it. If you take an
average human mind while still young, before the objects
it has chosen in life have given it a turn in any bad direction, you will generally find it desiring what is good, right,
and for the benefit of all; and if that season is properly used
to implant the knowledge and give the training which shall
render rectitude of judgment more habitual than sophistry,
a serious barrier will have been erected against the inroads
of selfishness and falsehood. Still, it is a very imperfect
education which trains the intelligence only, but not the
will. No one can dispense with an education directed expressly to the moral as well as the intellectual part of his
being. Such education, so far as it is direct, is either moral
or religious; and these may either be treated as distinct, or
as different aspects of the same thing. The subject we are
now considering is not education as a whole, but scholastic
education, and we must keep in view the inevitable limitations of what schools and universities can do. It is beyond
their power to educate morally or religiously. Moral and
religious education consist in training the feelings and
the daily habits; and these are, in the main, beyond the
sphere and inaccessible to the control of public education.
It is the home, the family, which gives us the moral or
religious education we really receive: and this is completed,
and modified, sometimes for the better, often for the worse,
by society, and the opinions and feelings with which we
are there surrounded. The moral or religious influence
which an university can exercise, consists less in any express
teaching, than in the pervading tone of the place. Whatever
it teaches, it should teach as penetrated by a sense of duty;
it should present all knowledge as chiefly a means to
worthiness of life, given for the double purpose of making

each of us practically useful to his fellow-creatures, and of elevating the character of the species itself; exalting and dignifying our nature. There is nothing which spreads more contagiously from teacher to pupil than elevation of sentiment: often and often have students caught from the living influence of a professor, a contempt for mean and selfish objects, and a noble ambition to leave the world better than they found it, which they have carried with them throughout life. In these respects, teachers of every kind have natural and peculiar means of doing with effect, what every one who mixes with his fellow-beings, or addresses himself to them in any character, should feel bound to do to the extent of his capacity and opportunities. What is special to an university on these subjects belongs chiefly, like the rest of its work, to the intellectual department. An university exists for the purpose of laying open to each succeeding generation, as far as the conditions of the case admit, the accumulated treasure of the thoughts of mankind. As an indispensable part of this, it has to make known to them what mankind at large, their own country, and the best and wisest individual men, have thought on the great subjects of morals and religion. There should be, and there is in most universities, professorial instruction in moral philosophy; but I could wish that this instruction were of a somewhat different type from what is ordinarily met with. I could wish that it were more expository, less polemical, and above all less dogmatic. The learner should be made acquainted with the principal systems of moral philosophy which have existed and been practically operative among mankind, and should hear what there is to be said for each: the Aristotelian, the Epicurean, the Stoic, the Judaic, the Christian in the various modes of its interpretation, which differ almost as much from one another as the teachings of those earlier schools. He should

184 J. S. MILL'S INAUGURAL ADDRESS

be made familiar with the different standards of right and
wrong which have been taken as the basis of ethics: general
utility, natural justice, natural rights, a moral sense, principles of practical reason, and the rest. Among all these, it
is not so much the teacher's business to take a side, and
fight stoutly for some one against the rest, as it is to direct
them all towards the establishment and preservation of the
rules of conduct most advantageous to mankind. There is
not one of these systems which has not its good side; not
one from which there is not something to be learnt by the
votaries of the others; not one which is not suggested by
a keen, though it may not always be a clear, perception of
some important truths, which are the prop of the system,
and the neglect or undervaluing of which in other systems
is their characteristic infirmity. A system which may be
as a whole erroneous, is still valuable, until it has forced
upon mankind a sufficient attention to the portion of truth
which suggested it. The ethical teacher does his part best,
when he points out how each system may be strengthened
even on its own basis, by taking into more complete account
the truths which other systems have realized more fully
and made more prominent. I do not mean that he should
encourage an essentially sceptical eclecticism. While placing
every system in the best aspect it admits of, and endeavouring to draw from all of them the most salutary
consequences compatible with their nature, I would by no
means debar him from enforcing by his best arguments his
own preference for some one of the number. They cannot
be all true; though those which are false as theories may
contain particular truths, indispensable to the completeness
of the true theory. But on this subject, even more than
on any of those I have previously mentioned, it is not the
teacher's business to impose his own judgment, but to inform
and discipline that of his pupil.

And this same clue, if we keep hold of it, will guide us through the labyrinth of conflicting thought into which we enter when we touch the great question of the relation of education to religion. As I have already said, the only really effective religious education is the parental—that of home and childhood. All that social and public education has in its power to do, further than by a general pervading tone of reverence and duty, amounts to little more than the information which it can give; but this is extremely valuable. I shall not enter into the question which has been debated with so much vehemence in the last and present generation, whether religion ought to be taught at all in universities and public schools, seeing that religion is the subject of all others on which men's opinions are most widely at variance. On neither side of this controversy do the disputants seem to me to have sufficiently freed their minds from the old notion of education, that it consists in the dogmatic inculcation from authority, of what the teacher deems true. Why should it be impossible, that information of the greatest value, on subjects connected with religion, should be brought before the student's mind; that he should be made acquainted with so important a part of the national thought, and of the intellectual labours of past generations, as those relating to religion, without being taught dogmatically the doctrines of any church or sect? Christianity being a historical religion, the sort of religious instruction which seems to me most appropriate to an University is the study of ecclesiastical history. If teaching, even on matters of scientific certainty, should aim quite as much at showing how the results are arrived at, as at teaching the results themselves, far more, then, should this be the case on subjects where there is the widest diversity of opinion among men of equal ability, and who have taken equal pains to arrive at the truth. This diversity should of itself be a warning to a conscientious teacher that he has no right to impose his opinion authoritatively upon a youthful mind. His teaching should not be in the spirit of dogmatism, but in that of enquiry. The pupil should not be addressed as if his religion had been chosen for him, but as one who will have to choose it for himself. The various Churches, established and unestablished, are quite competent to the task which is peculiarly theirs, that of teaching each its own doctrines, as far as necessary, to its own rising generation. The proper business of an University is different: not to tell us from authority what we ought to believe, and make us accept the belief as a duty, but to give us information and training, and help us to form our own belief in a manner worthy of intelligent beings, who seek for truth at all hazards, and demand to know all the difficulties, in order that they may be better qualified to find, or recognise, the most satisfactory mode of resolving them. The vast importance of these questions—the great results as regards the conduct of our lives, which depend upon our choosing one belief or another—are the strongest reasons why we should not trust our judgment when it has been formed in ignorance of the evidence, and why we should not consent to be restricted to a one-sided teaching, which informs us of what a particular teacher or association of teachers receive as true doctrine and sound argument, but of nothing more.

I do not affirm that an University, if it represses free thought and enquiry, must be altogether a failure, for the freest thinkers have often been trained in the most slavish seminaries of learning. The great Christian reformers were taught in Roman Catholic Universities; the sceptical philosophers of France were mostly educated by the Jesuits. The human mind is sometimes impelled all the more violently in one direction, by an over zealous and demon-

ıve attempt to drag it in the opposite. But this is not
ıat Universities are appointed for—to drive men from
them, even into good, by excess of evil. An University
ought to be a place of free speculation. The more diligently
it does its duty in all other respects, the more certain it is
to be that. The old English Universities, in the present
generation, are doing better work than they have done
within human memory in teaching the ordinary studies of
their curriculum; and one of the consequences has been,
that whereas they formerly seemed to exist mainly for the
repression of independent thought, and the chaining up of
the individual intellect and conscience, they are now the
great foci of free and manly enquiry, to the higher and
professional classes, south of the Tweed. The ruling minds
of those ancient seminaries have at last remembered that
to place themselves in hostility to the free use of the understanding, is to abdicate their own best privilege, that of
guiding it. A modest deference, at least provisional, to the
united authority of the specially instructed, is becoming in
a youthful and imperfectly formed mind; but when there
is no united authority—when the specially instructed are
so divided and scattered that almost any opinion can boast
of some high authority, and no opinion whatever can claim
all; when, therefore, it can never be deemed extremely
improbable that one who uses his mind freely may see
reason to change his first opinion; then, whatever you do,
keep, at all risks, your minds open: do not barter away
your freedom of thought. Those of you who are destined
for the clerical profession are, no doubt, so far held to a
certain number of doctrines, that if they ceased to believe
them they would not be justified in remaining in a position
in which they would be required to teach insincerely. But
use your influence to make those doctrines as few as
possible. It is not right that men should be bribed to hold

out against conviction—to shut their ears against objections, or, if the objections penetrate, to continue professing full and unfaltering belief when their confidence is already shaken. Neither is it right that if men honestly profess to have changed some of their religious opinions, their honesty should as a matter of course exclude them from taking a part for which they may be admirably qualified, in the spiritual instruction of the nation. The tendency of the age, on both sides of the ancient Border, is towards the relaxation of formularies, and a less rigid construction of articles. This very circumstance, by making the limits of orthodoxy less definite, and obliging every one to draw the line for himself, is an embarrassment to consciences. But I hold entirely with those clergymen who elect to remain in the national church, so long as they are able to accept its articles and confessions in any sense or with any interpretation consistent with common honesty, whether it be the generally received interpretation or not. If all were to desert the church who put a large and liberal construction on its terms of communion, or who would wish to see those terms widened, the national provision for religious teaching and worship would be left utterly to those who take the narrowest, the most literal, and purely textual view of the formularies; who, though by no means necessarily bigots, are under the great disadvantage of having the bigots for their allies, and who, however great their merits may be, and they are often very great, yet if the church is improvable, are not the most likely persons to improve it. Therefore, if it were not an impertinence in me to tender advice in such a matter, I should say, let all who conscientiously can, remain in the church. A church is far more easily improved from within than from without. Almost all the illustrious reformers of religion began by being clergymen: but they did not think that their profession as clergymen was inconsistent with being reformers. They mostly indeed ended their days outside the churches in which they were born; but it was because the churches, in an evil hour for themselves, cast them out. They did not think it any business of theirs to withdraw. They thought they had a better right to remain in the fold, than those had who expelled them.

I have now said what I had to say on the two kinds of education which the system of schools and universities is intended to promote—intellectual education, and moral education: knowledge and the training of the knowing faculty, conscience and that of the moral faculty. These are the two main ingredients of human culture; but they do not exhaust the whole of it. There is a third division, which, if subordinate, and owing allegiance to the two others, is barely inferior to them, and not less needful to the completeness of the human being; I mean the æsthetic branch; the culture which comes through poetry and art, and may be described as the education of the feelings, and the cultivation of the beautiful. This department of things deserves to be regarded in a far more serious light than is the custom of these countries. It is only of late, and chiefly by a superficial imitation of foreigners, that we have begun to use the word Art by itself, and to speak of Art as we speak of Science, or Government, or Religion: we used to talk of the Arts, and more specifically of the Fine Arts: and even by them were vulgarly meant only two forms of art, Painting and Sculpture, the two which as a people we cared least about—which were regarded even by the more cultivated among us as little more than branches of domestic ornamentation, a kind of elegant upholstery. The very words "Fine Arts" called up a notion of frivolity, of great pains expended on a rather trifling object—on something which differed from the cheaper and commoner arts of producing pretty things, mainly by being more difficult, and by giving fops an opportunity of pluming themselves on caring for it and on being able to talk about it. This estimate extended in no small degree, though not altogether, even to poetry; the queen of arts, but, in Great Britain, hardly included under the name. It cannot exactly be said that poetry was little thought of; we were proud of our Shakespeare and Milton, and in one period at least of our history, that of Queen Anne, it was a high literary distinction to be a poet; but poetry was hardly looked upon in any serious light, or as having much value except as an amusement or excitement, the superiority of which over others principally consisted in being that of a more refined order of minds. Yet the celebrated saying of Fletcher of Saltoun, "Let who will make the laws of a people if I write their songs," might have taught us how great an instrument for acting on the human mind we were undervaluing. It would be difficult for anybody to imagine that "Rule Britannia," for example, or "Scots wha hae," had no permanent influence on the higher region of human character; some of Moore's songs have done more for Ireland than all Grattan's speeches: and songs are far from being the highest or most impressive form of poetry. On these subjects, the mode of thinking and feeling of other countries was not only not intelligible, but not credible, to an average Englishman. To find Art ranking on a complete equality, in theory at least, with Philosophy, Learning, and Science—as holding an equally important place among the agents of civilization and among the elements of the worth of humanity; to find even painting and sculpture treated as great social powers, and the art of a country as a feature in its character and condition, little inferior in importance to either its religion or its government; all this only did not amaze and puzzle Englishmen, because it was too strange for them to be able to realize it, or, in truth, to believe it possible: and the radical difference of feeling on this matter between the British people and those of France, Germany, and the Continent generally, is one among the causes of that extraordinary inability to understand one another, which exists between England and the rest of Europe, while it does not exist to anything like the same degree between one nation of Continental Europe and another. It may be traced to the two influences which have chiefly shaped the British character since the days of the Stuarts: commercial money-getting business, and religious Puritanism. Business, demanding the whole of the faculties, and whether pursued from duty or the love of gain, regarding as a loss of time whatever does not conduce directly to the end; Puritanism, which looking upon every feeling of human nature, except fear and reverence for God, as a snare, if not as partaking of sin, looked coldly, if not disapprovingly, on the cultivation of the sentiments. Different causes have produced different effects in the Continental nations; among whom it is even now observable that virtue and goodness are generally for the most part an affair of the sentiments, while with us they are almost exclusively an affair of duty. Accordingly, the kind of advantage which we have had over many other countries in point of morals—I am not sure that we are not losing it—has consisted in greater tenderness of conscience. In this we have had on the whole a real superiority, though one principally negative; for conscience is with most men a power chiefly in the way of restraint—a power which acts rather in staying our hands from any great wickedness, than by the direction it gives to the general course of our desires and sentiments. One of the commonest types of character among us is that of a man all whose ambition is self-regarding; who has no higher purpose in life than to enrich or raise in the world himself and his family; who never dreams of making the good of his fellow-creatures or of his country an habitual object, further than giving away, annually or from time to time, certain sums in charity; but who has a conscience sincerely alive to whatever is generally considered wrong, and would scruple to use any very illegitimate means for attaining his self-interested objects. While it will often happen in other countries that men whose feelings and whose active energies point strongly in an unselfish direction, who have the love of their country, of human improvement, of human freedom, even of virtue, in great strength, and of whose thoughts and activity a large share is devoted to disinterested objects, will yet, in the pursuit of these or of any other objects that they strongly desire, permit themselves to do wrong things which the other man, though intrinsically, and taking the whole of his character, farther removed from what a human being ought to be, could not bring himself to commit. It is of no use to debate which of these two states of mind is the best, or rather the least bad. It is quite possible to cultivate the conscience and the sentiments too. Nothing hinders us from so training a man that he will not, even for a disinterested purpose, violate the moral law, and also feeding and encouraging those high feelings, on which we mainly rely for lifting men above low and sordid objects, and giving them a higher conception of what constitutes success in life. If we wish men to practise virtue, it is worth while trying to make them love virtue, and feel it an object in itself, and not a tax paid for leave to pursue other objects. It is worth training them to feel, not only actual wrong or actual meanness, but the absence of noble aims and endeavours, as not merely blameable but also degrading: to have a feeling of the miserable smallness of mere self in the face of this great universe, of the collective mass of our fellow creatures, in the face of past history and of the indefinite future—the poorness and insignificance of human life if it is to be all spent in making things comfortable for ourselves and our kin, and raising ourselves and them a step or two on the social ladder. Thus feeling, we learn to respect ourselves only so far as we feel capable of nobler objects: and if unfortunately those by whom we are surrounded do not share our aspirations, perhaps disapprove the conduct to which we are prompted by them— to sustain ourselves by the ideal sympathy of the great characters in history, or even in fiction, and by the contemplation of an idealized posterity: shall I add, of ideal perfection embodied in a Divine Being? Now, of this elevated tone of mind the great source of inspiration is poetry, and all literature so far as it is poetical and artistic. We may imbibe exalted feelings from Plato, or Demosthenes, or Tacitus, but it is in so far as those great men are not solely philosophers or orators or historians, but poets and artists. Nor is it only loftiness, only the heroic feelings, that are bred by poetic cultivation. Its power is as great in calming the soul as in elevating it—in fostering the milder emotions, as the more exalted. It brings home to us all those aspects of life which take hold of our nature on its unselfish side, and lead us to identify our joy and grief with the good or ill of the system of which we form a part; and all those solemn or pensive feelings, which, without having any direct application to conduct, incline us to take life seriously, and predispose us to the reception of anything which comes before us in the shape of duty. Who does not feel a better man after a course of Dante, or of Wordsworth, or, I will add, of Lucretius or the *Georgics*, or after brooding over Gray's *Elegy*, or Shelley's *Hymn to Intellectual Beauty?* I have spoken of poetry, but all the other modes of art produce similar effects in their degree. The races and nations whose senses are naturally finer and their sensuous perceptions more exercised than ours, receive the same kind of impressions from painting and sculpture: and many of the more delicately organized among ourselves do the same. All the arts of expression tend to keep alive and in activity the feelings they express. Do you think that the great Italian painters would have filled the place they did in the European mind, would have been universally ranked among the greatest men of their time, if their productions had done nothing for it but to serve as the decoration of a public hall or a private *salon*? Their Nativities and Crucifixions, their glorious Madonnas and Saints, were to their susceptible Southern countrymen the great school not only of devotional, but of all the elevated and all the imaginative feelings. We colder Northerns may approach to a conception of this function of art when we listen to an oratorio of Handel, or give ourselves up to the emotions excited by a Gothic cathedral. Even apart from any specific emotional expression, the mere contemplation of beauty of a high order produces in no small degree this elevating effect on the character. The power of natural scenery addresses itself to the same region of human nature which corresponds to Art. There are few capable of feeling the sublimer order of natural beauty, such as your own Highlands and other mountain regions afford, who are not, at least temporarily, raised by it above the littlenesses of humanity, and made to feel the puerility of the petty objects which set men's interests at variance, contrasted with the nobler pleasures which all might share. To whatever avocations we may be called in life, let us never quash these susceptibilities within us, but carefully seek the opportunities of maintaining them in exercise. The more prosaic our ordinary duties, the more necessary it is to keep up the tone of our minds by frequent visits to that higher region of thought and feeling, in which every work seems dignified in proportion to the ends for which, and the spirit in which, it is done; where we learn, while eagerly seizing every opportunity of exercising higher faculties and performing higher duties, to regard all useful and honest work as a public function, which may be ennobled by the mode of performing it— which has not properly any other nobility than what that gives—and which, if ever so humble, is never mean but when it is meanly done, and when the motives from which it is done are mean motives. There is, besides, a natural affinity between goodness and the cultivation of the Beautiful, when it is real cultivation, and not a mere unguided instinct. He who has learnt what beauty is, if he be of a virtuous character, will desire to realize it in his own life— will keep before himself a type of perfect beauty in human character, to light his attempts at self-culture. There is a true meaning in the saying of Goethe, though liable to be misunderstood and perverted, that the Beautiful is greater than the Good; for it includes the Good, and adds something to it: it is the Good made perfect, and fitted with all the collateral perfections which make it a finished and completed thing. Now, this sense of perfection, which would make us demand from every creation of man the very utmost that it ought to give, and render us intolerant of the smallest fault in ourselves or in anything we do, is one of the results of Art cultivation. No other human productions come so near to perfection as works of pure Art. In all other things, we are, and may reasonably be, satisfied if the degree of excellence is as great as the object immediately in view seems to us to be worth: but in Art, the perfection is itself the object. If I were to define Art, I should be inclined to call it, the endeavour after perfection in execution. If we meet with even a piece of mechanical work which bears the marks of being done in this spirit—which is done as if the workman loved it, and tried to make it as good as possible, though something less good would have answered the purpose for which it was ostensibly made—we say that he has worked like an artist. Art, when really cultivated, and not merely practised empirically, maintains, what it first gave the conception of, an ideal Beauty, to be eternally aimed at, though surpassing what can be actually attained; and by this idea it trains us never to be completely satisfied with imperfection in what we ourselves do and are: to idealize, as much as possible, every work we do, and most of all, our own characters and lives.

And now, having travelled with you over the whole range of the materials and training which an University supplies as a preparation for the higher uses of life, it is almost needless to add any exhortation to you to profit by the gift. Now is your opportunity for gaining a degree of insight into subjects larger and far more ennobling than the minutiæ of a business or a profession, and for acquiring a facility of using your minds on all that concerns the higher interests of man, which you will carry with you into the occupations of active life, and which will prevent even the short intervals of time which that may leave you, from being altogether lost for noble purposes. Having once conquered the first difficulties, the only ones of which the irksomeness surpasses the interest; having turned the point beyond which what was once a task becomes a pleasure; in even the busiest after-life, the higher powers of your mind will make progress imperceptibly, by the spontaneous exercise of your thoughts, and by the lessons you will know how to learn from daily experience. So, at least, it will be if in your early studies you have fixed your eyes upon the ultimate end from which those studies take their chief value—that of making you more effective combatants in the great fight which never ceases to rage between Good and Evil, and more equal to coping with the ever new problems which the changing course of human nature and human society present to be resolved. Aims like these commonly retain the footing which they have once established in the mind; and their presence in our thoughts keeps our higher faculties in exercise, and makes us consider the acquirements and powers which we store up at any time of our lives, as a mental capital, to be freely expended in helping forward any mode which presents itself of making mankind in any respect wiser or better, or placing any portion of human affairs on a more sensible and rational footing than its existing one. There is not one of us who may not qualify himself so to improve the average amount of opportunities, as to leave his fellow creatures some little the better for the use he has known how to make of his intellect. To make this little greater, let us strive to keep ourselves acquainted with the best thoughts that are brought forth by the original minds of the age; that we may know what movements stand most in need of our aid, and that, as far as depends on us, the good seed may not fall on a rock, and perish without reaching the soil in which it might have germinated and flourished. You are to be a part of the public who are to welcome, encourage, and help forward the future intellectual benefactors of humanity; and you are, if possible, to furnish your contingent to the number of those benefactors. Nor let any one be discouraged by what may seem, in moments of despondency, the lack of time and of opportunity. Those who know how to employ opportunities will often find that they can create them: and what we achieve depends less on the amount of time we possess, than on the use we make of our time. You and your like are the hope and resource of your country in the coming generation. All great things which that generation is destined to do, have to be done by some like you; several will assuredly be done by persons for whom society has done much less, to whom it has given far less preparation, than those whom I am now addressing. I do not attempt to instigate you by the prospect of direct rewards, either earthly or heavenly; the less we think about being rewarded in either way, the better for us. But there is one reward which will not fail you, and which may be called disinterested, because it is not a consequence, but is inherent in the very fact of deserving it; the deeper and more varied interest you will feel in life: which will give it tenfold its value, and a value which will last to the end. All merely personal objects grow less valuable as we advance in life: this not only endures but increases.

NOTES

EDUCATION

James Mill's article on Education was published in the Supplement to the 5th edition of the *Encyclopaedia Britannica* (edited by Macvey Napier). Bain (*James Mill*, p. 247) says that it must have been written in 1818. It was reprinted in 1828 along with the articles on Government, Jurisprudence, Liberty of the Press, Prisons, Colonies, and the Law of Nations, in a small paper-covered volume, not for sale; from this the present reprint has been made (with the correction of a few obvious misprints, particularly in the French quotations). This was the volume reviewed by Macaulay in the *Edinburgh Magazine* (March, June, October, 1829); out of respect for Mill he did not include these articles in his collected essays, though they may be found in his miscellaneous writings. Mill's articles were evidently read widely; he said in 1825 that they were "the text-books of the young men of the Union at Cambridge." They were reprinted by Roebuck in 1836 as a part of his series "Pamphlets for the People"; the "Education" was sold for 4*d*. Bain says that the circulation of the tracts is stated to have reached ten thousand, but does not specify the number sold of each (*op. cit.* p. 398).

Section I

p. 7. **called ideas of sense:** we now call them images.

p. 8. **David Hartley (1705–57),** a medical practitioner, developed a physiological psychology in his *Observations on Man* (1749). In this work he explains sensation as due to vibrations of the nerves, and memory as due to slighter vibrations (or vibratiuncles); these latter are aroused by association. Mill adopted his views on association, but not their physiological explanation. It is interesting to notice that Mill's attitude towards Hartley underwent exactly the opposite process to Coleridge's: he came to admire him after meeting Bentham. But Coleridge, who at first hailed him as "of mortal kind wisest" and called his eldest son after him (1796), by 1817 had completely turned round, and devoted a chapter of *Biographia Literaria* to proving "that Hartley's system...is neither tenable in theory nor founded in facts."

Hartley's followers in England included, besides the Utilitarians, Joseph Priestley, the chemist, who republished Hartley's book in 1775.

Etienne de Condillac (1750–80): his earliest work, *Essai sur l'origine des connaissances humaines,* was published in 1746, three years before Hartley's *Observations* (cf. p. 15). His most important book, *Traité des sensations,* appeared in 1754; in this he derived the whole mental life from sensations. The most famous part of his work is that in which he imagines a human soul imprisoned in a marble statue and gradually developing organs of sense. His followers in France were Bonnet (1720–93), a Swiss naturalist; Destutt de Tracy (1754–1836) and Pierre Cabanis (1757–1808). For Cabanis, see note on p. 30.

Dr. Reid: Thomas Reid (1710–92), founder of the "Scottish" school of "common sense," held that we can apprehend the external world by immediate intuition. His "followers" were Dugald Stewart (1753–1828), under whom Mill studied at Edinburgh; Thomas Brown (1778–1856); and Sir William Hamilton (1778–1856). Kant was never appreciated truly by Mill; he writes to Place (8 Oct. 1816): "I am reading, at least I have begun to read the Critic of Pure Reason. I see clearly enough what poor Kant is about... Hartley's is the true scent." (cit. Halévy, vol. III, p. 460.)

p. 12. Mr. Hobbs: Thomas Hobbes (1588–1679), the author of *Leviathan;* his *Human Nature* was published in 1650.

p. 13. Mr. Locke: the passage is quoted from the *Essay on the Human Understanding,* book II, chap. xxxiii, sect. 5 ("Of the Association of Ideas").

p. 14. Mr. Hume: David Hume (1711–76). Of his *Treatise of Human Nature* (published anonymously in 1739) he says: "Never literary attempt was more unfortunate. It fell *deadborn from the press* without reaching such a distinction as even to excite a murmur among the zealots." (*My own Life.*)

Section II

p. 23. the four cardinal virtues, etc.: cf. Bentham, "since the time of Aristotle, four virtues, Prudence, Fortitude, Temperance, and Justice, have taken the names of the cardinal virtues.... In Aristotle's catalogue the virtue of benevolence—effective benevolence—is forgotten, and there is nothing in its stead but justice, which is but a portion of benevolence in disguise." (*Deontology,* cit. Halévy, vol. III, p. 310.)

Section III

p. 24. **Happiness, the End,** etc.: for an acute criticism of the Utilitarian position from the Catholic standpoint, see Sir Thomas Wyse's *Education Reform* (1836), p. 36.

p. 25. **They affirm,** etc.: the philosophers holding the various ethical theories are as follows: "a peculiar sense," Hutcheson and Shaftesbury; "the faculty which discerns pure truth," Clarke and Cudworth; "common sense," Reid; "the notion of the fitness and unfitness of things," Price; "the law of nature," probably Butler; "truth," Wollaston; "one eminent philosopher...truth," Mill means either Hume or Adam Smith (*Theory of Moral Sentiments*). Hume maintained that "morality is determined by sentiment," and defined virtue as "whatever mental action or quality gives to a spectator the pleasing sentiment of approbation, and vice the contrary"; this "sentiment" Adam Smith investigated more closely, and found to be the sympathy of an impartial observer.

Section IV

p. 26. **Helvetius:** Claude Adrien Helvétius (1715–71), one of the minor encyclopaedists. As a young man he was farmer-general and chamberlain to the Queen of France; but he spent most of his life in retirement on his estate, writing philosophical and other works. His *De l'esprit* was publicly burnt in 1759; for this reason he did not permit his *De l'homme, de ses facultés intellectuelles, et de son éducation* (the work to which Mill principally refers) to appear until after his death (1772). His work is now so dead that Mill's eulogy strikes us as strangely extravagant. His conclusions were attacked by Rousseau in the *Nouvelle Héloïse* and in *Emile*; Section v of *De l'homme* contains Helvétius' rejoinder.

p. 28. **The works of Helvetius...these circumstances:** see e.g. sect. i, chap. ii: "C'est à l'instant même où l'enfant reçoit le mouvement et la vie, qu'il reçoit ses premières instructions. C'est quelquefois dans les flancs où il est conçu qu'il apprend à connoître l'état de maladie et de santé. Cependant la mère accouche: l'enfant s'agite, pousse des cris; la faim l'échauffe; il sent un besoin; ce besoin desserre ses lèvres, lui fait saisir et sucer avidement le sein nourricier. Quelques mois s'écoulent, ses yeux se dessillent, ses organes se fortifient: ils deviennent peu-à-peu susceptibles de toutes les impressions. Alors le sens de la vue, de l'ouïe, du goût, du toucher, de l'odorat, enfin toutes les portes de son âme sont ouvertes. Alors tous les objets de la nature s'y précipitent en foule et gravent une infinité d'idées dans sa mémoire. Dans ces premiers moments quels peuvent être les vrais instituteurs de l'enfance? les diverses sensations qu'elle éprouve. Ce sont autant d'instructions qu'elle reçoit.

"A-t-on donné à deux enfants le même précepteur, leur a-t-il appris à distinguer leurs lettres, à lire, à reciter leur catéchisme etc.? on croit leur avoir donné la même éducation. Le philosophe en juge autrement. Selon lui les vrais précepteurs de l'enfance sont les objets qui l'environnent: c'est à ces Instituteurs qu'elle doit presque toutes ses idées."

p. 27. **Sir William Jones (1746–94),** the Sanskrit scholar, a friend of Johnson, Gibbon, and Burke. Teignmouth adds: "The assertion (which I do not admit) will remind the reader of the modest declaration of Sir Isaac Newton, that, if he had done the world any service, it was due to nothing but industry and patient thought."

p. 30. **Pierre Cabanis (1757–1808),** a follower of Condillac, developed the physiological side of his teaching; he held that external impressions were transformed into sensations (or perceptions, as we should now call them) in the brain. His *Rapports du Physique et du Moral de l'Homme* appeared in 1802.

Dr. Darwin: Erasmus Darwin (1731–1802), grandfather of Charles Darwin, was a physician and biologist. His *Zoonomia, the Laws of Organic Life* (1794–6), is partly medical (it contains an elaborate classification of diseases); but Mill's interest lay in the philosophical part, in which Darwin extends the physiological side of Hartley's system (see esp. part I, sect. x, "Of Associate Motions"). Erasmus Darwin was one of the pioneers of evolution, his attitude being Lamarckian: his grandson's great contribution was the theory of natural selection by means of variations. Charles Darwin in his *Autobiography* says that *Zoonomia* disappointed him, "the proportion of speculation being so large to the facts given"; but he thinks that his early reading of the book may have influenced him. The cause of Erasmus Darwin was championed by Samuel Butler. His poem, "Loves of the Plants," was parodied as "Loves of the Triangles" by Canning in the *Anti-Jacobin*.

p. 42. **Cabanis:** the quotation is from his first Mémoire. The eighth treats at length "De l'influence du régime sur les dispositions et les habitudes morales."

p. 45. **Dr. Crichton:** Sir Alexander Crichton (1763–1856), who became physician to the Czar Alexander I, and a very important man in Russia. His book on *Mental Derangement* appeared in 1798.

p. 46. Dr. Smith: the reference is to *Wealth of Nations*, bk. v, chap. i: "In the progress of the division of labour, the employment of the far greater part of those who live by labour, that is, of the great body of the people, comes to be confined to a few very simple operations; frequently to one or two." This striking passage is all the more interesting in the present conditions of industry; see e.g. Henry Ford, *My Life and Work*.

p. 54. Miss Edgeworth: Maria Edgeworth (1767–1849); Mill probably refers to her *Moral Tales* (1801).

p. 57. An anecdote: I have been unable to find any corroboration of this story.

p. 61. Hume: the reference is perhaps to the essay *Of National Characters*.

p. 63. Chrestomathia: Bentham explains the name in a footnote: "From a Greek word signifying *useful learning*: the English word found in an English book of the 17th century." Subjects were to be taught in the order of utility, classics being omitted. The fees were to be £6 per annum.

the Baptist Missionaries in India: Mill knew of them from William Allen, the Quaker, with whom he collaborated in educational schemes; it was in Allen's periodical *The Philanthropist* that Mill's *Schools for All* first appeared. Allen writes to him (18th of 9th month, 1815): "The Baptists have finally resolved to make education the basis of their missionary plans in the East Indies" (Bain, *op. cit.* p. 149). Mill was no doubt glad to show that Dr Andrew Bell was not the only enlightened educationist who had worked in India.

p. 67. There are several causes, etc.: cf. Adam Smith's remarks on the evils of educational endowments, *op. cit.* bk. v, chap. i, part 3.

D'Alembert: J. B. Dalembert (1717–83), mathematician and editor of the *Encyclopaedia*. His *Sur la Destruction des Jésuites en France, par un Auteur désintéressé*, appeared in 1765. The passage quoted continues: "et qui n'ont cessé que par l'état où sont tombés ces ordres devenus incapable d'exciter l'envie."

Wolf: Christian Wolff of Marburg; the quotation is from his *Philosophia Rationalis sive Logica* (1728).

AUTOBIOGRAPHY

Mainly "written or revised previous to, or during the year 1861," the last chapter was finished off in 1870. Mill died in 1873; the *Autobiography* was published the same year. It was edited by Helen Taylor, his step-daughter and secretary. Chapters I and II, and a part of chapter V, are here printed.

For fuller and more accurate details of James Mill's early life, see Bain's *James Mill*, chap. I. It is interesting to note that he acted as tutor to Wilhelmina, daughter of Sir John Stuart (after whom his eldest son was named); she was the object of Scott's first, but unsuccessful, love.

p. 114. Bain (*John Stuart Mill*, pp. 16 sqq.) gives a summary of a diary kept by Mill during his stay in France. Here is a typical passage: "July 4th. Rose at 5; home from bathing, &c., at $7\frac{1}{2}$. Has obtained Voltaire's Essai sur les Moeurs, which he includes amongst his stated reading; breakfast at $\frac{1}{4}$ to 9: at $9\frac{1}{2}$, begins Voltaire where he left off in England, reads six chapters in two hours; Virgil's Georgics, 47 lines; at $12\frac{1}{4}$ began a treatise on French Adverbs; at $1\frac{1}{2}$, began the second book of Legendre (Geometry), read the definitions and five propositions; miscellaneous employments till 3, then took second music-lesson. Dined; Family again to Franconi's, but he could not give up his dancing-lesson; this got, he writes French exercises and practises music. July 5th. Rose at 5; too rainy for bathing. Five chapters of Voltaire: from $7\frac{1}{2}$ till $8\frac{1}{2}$, Mr. G. corrects his French exercises which had got into arrears as regards correction; Music-master came; at $9\frac{1}{2}$ began new exercise (French); puts his room in order; at $11\frac{1}{4}$ took out Lucian and finished Necyomantia; five propositions of Legendre, renewed expressions of his superiority to all other geometers; practises Music-lessons; Thomson's Chemistry, makes out various Chemical Tables, the drift not explained; at $3\frac{1}{4}$, tries several propositions in West, and made out two that he had formerly failed in; begins a table of 58 rivers in France, to show what departments each passes through, and the chief towns on their banks; 4, dined; finishes Chemical Table; dancing-lesson; supped. Reports that a distinguished music-mistress is engaged, at whose house he is to have instrumental practice."

p. 118. **this time:** Mill's narrative (in the portion omitted) had reached the year 1828.

The *Westminster Review* was a radical organ, established as a counterblast to the *Edinburgh* and *Quarterly* by Bentham in 1823. Both Mills contributed several articles. It was edited by (Sir) John Bowring.

p. 120. Coleridge's "Dejection": evidently quoted from memory, as there are slight errors. The quotation on p. 124 is from *Lines composed 21 February, 1827*.

p. 124. Marmontel: poet, novelist, and encyclopaedist (1723–99). His *Mémoires d'un père à ses enfants* appeared in 1804, so that it was a recent publication when Mill read it. After describing how he heard at College of his father's death, and his dismal journey home, Marmontel continues: "J'arrive, au milieu de la nuit, à la porte de ma maison. Je frappe, je me nomme, et, dans le moment, un murmure plaintif, un mélange de voix gémissantes se fait entendre. Toute la famille se lève, on vient m'ouvrir; et, en entrant, je suis environné de cette famille éplorée; mère, enfants, vieilles femmes, tous presque nus, échevelés, semblables à des spectres, et me tendant les bras avec des cris qui percent et déchirent mon cœur. Je ne sais quelle force que la nature nous réserve, sans doute, pour le malheur extrême, se déploya tout-à-coup en moi. J'avais à soulever un poids énorme de douleur; je n'y succombai point. J'ouvris mes bras, mon sein à cette foule de malheureux; je les y reçus tous; et, avec l'assurance d'un homme inspiré par le Ciel, sans marquer de faiblesse, sans verser une larme, moi qui pleure facilement: 'Ma mère, mes frères, mes sœurs, nous éprouvons, leur dis-je, la plus grande des afflictions; ne nous y laissons point abattre. Mes enfants, vous perdez un père; vous en retrouvez un, je vous en servirai; je le suis, je veux l'être; j'en embrasse tous les devoirs; et vous n'êtes plus orphelins.' A ces mots, des ruisseaux de larmes, mais des larmes bien moins amères, coulèrent de leurs yeux. 'Ah! s'écria ma mère, en me pressant contre son cœur, mon fils! mon cher enfant! que je t'ai bien connu.' Et mes frères, mes sœurs, mes bonnes tantes, ma grand'mère, tombèrent à genoux."

p. 125. the anti-self-consciousness theory of Carlyle: set forth clearly, e.g. in his essay *Characteristics* (1831): "The healthy know not of their health, but only the sick: this is the Physician's Aphorism; and applicable in a far wider sense than he gives it. We may say, it holds no less in moral, intellectual, political, poetical, than in merely corporeal therapeutics; that wherever, or in what shape soever, powers of the sort which can be named *vital* are at work, herein lies the test of their working right or working wrong." The essay as a whole is an elaborate example of fallacious argument from analogy.

p. 127. Weber's *Oberon* had just appeared (1826).

INAUGURAL ADDRESS

p. 133. **It is not a place of professional education:** cf. Newman's *Idea of a University* (1852), esp. chap. vii.

p. 138. **that old controversy:** see Macaulay's *Essay on Sir William Temple*, Swift's *Battle of the Books*, and Jebb's *Bentley*.

Many educational reformers: Mill no doubt had Herbert Spencer particularly in mind; contrast the wider conceptions of Huxley, or those contained in Farrar's *Essays on a Liberal Education* (1867). But Mill's point of view had been anticipated by Sir Thomas Wyse, whose *Education Reform* (1836) deserves to be far better known than it is. He writes (p. 160): "Latin and Greek, it is urged, require the full allotment of time, which is actually expended upon their acquisition. Were this true, the only alternative which could be proposed would be, the sacrifice of one or other of these languages. But a sober examination into the case will prove, that, by a better arrangement of the period for commencing the classic languages, and by a better process in teaching them, not only time might easily be spared for these studies, without interfering with that of the languages, but that, in fact, the languages themselves would gain, instead of losing, and the pupil be enabled to attain a competent knowledge of Physics, and learn Greek and Latin much more efficiently besides." This is a position which Dr Arnold had not reached.

p. 139. **The only tolerable Latin grammars,** etc.: probably those by Thomas Ruddiman, whose *Rudiments of the Latin Tongue* (1714) "passed through fifteen editions during his lifetime, and long remained in use in the schools of Scotland" (Sandys, *History of Classical Scholarship*, II, 412). Kennedy's *Public School Latin Primer* (1866) had just been adopted by the public schools, to the disgust of many masters (see Bowen, in Farrar, *op. cit.* p. 196).

p. 142. **Archbishop Whately:** Richard Whately (1787–1863), one of the famous company of Fellows of Oriel (1811–22); afterwards Archbishop of Dublin; author of *Logic, Rhetoric*, etc.

p. 144. **it has always seemed to me,** etc.: Mill's view would have been shared by Robert Vaughan, Professor of History at University College, London (1833–39); see Bellot's *University*

College, London, p. 117. T. H. Key, headmaster of University College School, was "vehemently opposed to history" as a school subject, and substituted social science (*op. cit.* p. 170); in the same way Spencer advocated comparative sociology in its place.

p. 146. **"Words are the counters,"** etc.: "Words are wise mens counters, they do but reckon by them: but they are the mony of fooles." *Leviathan,* 1, iv, 15.

p. 150. **grammar...is the most elementary part of logic:** Jespersen, *Philosophy of Grammar,* p. 47, regards this passage as out of date, even for its age. "On the whole," he concludes, "we must not expect to arrive at a 'universal grammar' in the sense of the old philosophical grammarians." He shows later (p. 149) that the logical subject is not necessarily the same as the grammatical.

p. 154. **curiosa felicitas:** "praeterea curandum est, ne sententiae emineant extra corpus orationis expressae, sed intexto vestibus colore niteant. Homerus testis et lyrici Romanusque Vergilius et Horatii curiosa felicitas." Petronius, *Sat.* 118.

Swift's definition: "Proper words in proper places make the true definition of a style.... When a man's thoughts are clear, the properest words will generally offer themselves first, and his own judgement will direct him in what order to place them, so as they may be best understood" (Johnson's *Life of Swift,* ed. Birkbeck Hill, III, 65).

p. 156. **To what purpose...verses:** for a trenchant attack on "Greek and Latin Verse-Composition as a General Branch of Education," see F. W. Farrar in *Essays on a Liberal Education* (1867).

p. 164. **A well-known essay by Sir William Hamilton:** *On the Study of Mathematics as an Exercise of Mind* (*Edin. Rev.* Jan. 1836). Hamilton criticises Whewell, who claimed in his *Thoughts on the Study of Mathematics as a part of a Liberal Education* (1835) that "Mathematics are a means of forming logical habits better than Logic itself."

p. 170. **The defects of his conception,** etc.: Mill censures Bacon for assuming that "every object has an invariable co-existent" (*Logic,* bk. III, chap. xxii, 4), and for "entirely overlooking the Plurality of Causes" (*ib.* v, iii, 7). For a full criticism of Bacon's theory of Induction, see R. W. Church, *Bacon,* chap. viii.

p. 175. **Ferrier:** James Ferrier (1808–64), Professor of Moral Philosophy at St Andrews 1845–64. **Alexander Bain**

(1818–1903), Professor of Logic and English at Aberdeen (1862–80); a friend of Mill's, who developed the Utilitarian psychology and ethics; a systematic exponent of educational theory.

p. 179. **Mr. Austin:** John Austin (1790–1859), the first Professor of Jurisprudence at University College, London (1826–32), a man of great but unfulfilled ability; he was one of the Utilitarian group, and is discussed at length in Mill's *Autobiography*.

Mr. Maine: Sir Henry Maine (1822–88), the famous jurist; his *Ancient Law* was published in 1861.

p. 186. **I do not affirm,** etc.: "In the reception given to the Address, he was most struck with the vociferous applause of the Divinity students at the Free-thought passage. He was privately thanked by others among the hearers for this part." Bain, *op. cit.* p. 128.

p. 190. **Fletcher of Saltoun:** Andrew Fletcher (1655–1716), a Scottish patriot. This well-known quotation comes from *An Account of a Conversation concerning a Right Regulation of Governments for the common good of Mankind* (1704): "I knew a very wise man so much of Sir Christopher [Musgrave's] sentiment that he believed if a man were permitted to make all the ballads he need not care who should make the laws of a nation." The "very wise man" presumably had in mind Plato, *Republic*, 424.

p. 195. **the saying of Goethe:** I have been unable to trace this reference.

BIBLIOGRAPHY

I. GENERAL

The standard English book is Sir Leslie Stephen's *The English Utilitarians* (3 vols., London, 1900). This is supplemented by Elie Halévy, *La Formation du Radicalisme philosophique* (3 vols., Paris, 1901–4), translated by Mary Morris as *The Growth of Philosophic Radicalism* (London, 1928); vol. III, chap. ii is indispensable for a full understanding of the philosophy of Bentham and James Mill. An excellent short study is W. L. Davidson's *Political Thought in England: the Utilitarians* (Home University Library, 1915). W. B. Pillsbury, *The History of Psychology* (London, 1929) will also be found useful.

II. BIOGRAPHICAL, ETC.

The authoritative life of James Mill is that by Alexander Bain (London, 1882); as Stephen says, if rather dry, it deals with a dry subject. Bain published in the same year *John Stuart Mill, a Criticism: with Personal Recollections*. The whole of J. S. Mill's *Autobiography* should of course be read (reprinted in World's Classics). *The Letters of John Stuart Mill* (2 vols., London, 1910) contain much illuminating material, and most interesting introductions by Hugh Elliot and Mary Taylor (Mrs Mill's grand-daughter). W. L. Courtney's *Life of J. S. Mill* (London, 1889) is more readable than Bain's, but contains little that is new. See also *The Personal Life of George Grote*, by Mrs Grote (London, 1873), and the articles on James Mill in the *Penny Cyclopaedia* and *D.N.B.* For James Mill's educational activities see *The Life of Francis Place*, by Graham Wallas; *University College, London, 1826–1926*, by H. H. Bellot (London, 1929); and David Salmon's *Life of Joseph Lancaster* (also articles in the *Education Record*, Oct. 1913 and Feb. 1917). The sources are Mill's *Schools for All, in Preference to Schools for Churchmen only* (1812); Bentham's *Chrestomathia* (1816) and *Church-of-Englandism* (1818). John Stuart Mill deals with the question of national education in his essay *On Liberty* (1859), chap. v, "Applications."